In the Fiery Furnace of Suffering

Tabor Laughlin

WIPF & STOCK · Eugene, Oregon

IN THE FIERY FURNACE OF SUFFERING

Copyright © 2018 Tabor Laughlin. All rights reserved. Except for brief quotations in critical publications or reviews, no part of this book may be reproduced in any manner without prior written permission from the publisher. Write: Permissions, Wipf and Stock Publishers, 199 W. 8th Ave., Suite 3, Eugene, OR 97401.

Wipf & Stock
An Imprint of Wipf and Stock Publishers
199 W. 8th Ave., Suite 3
Eugene, OR 97401

www.wipfandstock.com

PAPERBACK ISBN: 978-1-5326-5410-7
HARDCOVER ISBN: 978-1-5326-5411-4
EBOOK ISBN: 978-1-5326-5412-1

Manufactured in the U.S.A.

In the Fiery Furnace of Suffering

To my college friend Scoop, whom the Lord used to teach me about God's purposes in our sufferings

These trials have come so that your faith—of greater worth than gold, which perishes even though refined by fire—may be proved genuine, and may result in praise, glory, and honor when Jesus Christ is revealed.

—1 Peter 1:7

Contents

Section I: Biblical Principles About Suffering | 1

Chapter 1—What's This Book About? | 3

This chapter covers how I first heard about the truth on God's sovereignty from a friend when we were backpacking around Europe in college. It also briefly introduces this book on suffering.

Chapter 2—Origin of Suffering | 6

Chapter 2 gives some clarity about the origin of suffering. The chapter looks at:

1. Job's Sufferings (1 Pet 1:7)
2. Lord, You Have Assigned Me My Portion and My Cup (Ps 16:5, 6; 139:16; 138:8; Isa 45:7; Exod 4:11)
3. Some Sufferings Are from the Enemy (1 Pet 5:8–10; Luke 22:31, 32; Eph 6:10–20; Neh 4:10–16)
4. Some Sufferings Are a Result of Our Own Sin (Reward for Obedience; Punishment for Disobedience—Lev 26)

Chapter 3—How to Suffer Well | 16

Chapter 3 uses biblical ideas for how we can suffer well. These would relate to how we should react when we are actually going through sufferings, not just after they are finished. Some of these ideas include:

CONTENTS

1. Remember God Delivers His People through Trials (Exod 14; Isa 43:1–3; Dan 3:17; Ps 124:1, 4, 5; Heb 10, 11, 12:1–3; 2 Tim 4:17, 18; 1 Sam 17:37)
2. Do Not Be Surprised at the Painful Trial You Are Suffering (1 Pet 4:12, 13; John 16:33)
3. We Must Go through Many Hardships to Enter the Kingdom of God (Acts 14:21–25; Rom 8:18; 2 Cor 4:17)
4. Rejoice in Your Sufferings (Jas 1:2, 3; Rom 5:3–5; Lam 3:19–21; 22–26; 2 Cor 12:10)
5. Sharing in Christ's Sufferings (Rom 8:17; Phil 3:10; 1 Pet 4:13; Acts 5:41)
6. Consider How Temporary Our Life Is (Ps 39:4; 2 Cor 4:16–18)

Chapter 4—Results of Suffering | 28

This chapter is about some results that come from suffering. What are some of God's purposes for our growth and sanctification as a result of our suffering? These would include:

1. God Refines Us in Our Sufferings (Rom 8:28; Isa 48:9–11; 1 Pet 1:7)
2. Suffering Increases Our Thirst for Heaven (2 Cor 4:16–18; John 14:1–6; 1 Thess 4:13–18)
3. When We Suffer, We Often Feel Closest to God (1 Pet 4:1, 2)
4. Comfort Others with the Comfort We Received from God (2 Cor 1:3–6)
5. We Are Forced to Rely More on God, Rather than on Ourselves (2 Cor 1:8, 9; 4:7–9; 1 Sam 30:3–6)

6 When We Suffer, We Are Greatly Blessed (Jas 1:12; Luke 21:17-19; Jas 5:10, 11; Ps 119:67, 71)

Section II: My Sufferings | 43

Introduction: Boasting in Sufferings (2 Cor 11:16-33; Rom 8:28; Isa 55:9; story of Joseph)

Chapter 5—Disease | 49

In this chapter I look into detail about some of my biggest personal sufferings, which came through my mother's genetic neurological disease and subsequent death from it, and then me getting tested positive to have the same neurological disease. I go through the important events in these stories, as well as things that the Lord has taught me so far from these two particular hardships related to disease.

1 Disease in Family (Rom 8:28; 2 Cor 1:3-6)

2 Getting Tested Positive for Huntington's Disease (Job 1:18-20; Rom 14:19, 20; John 12:27, 28; Phil 1:20-26; 2 Cor 12:7-10; Jas 4:14; Ps 39:4; Phil 1:5, 6; Jer 15:2; Job 14:6; John 21:19, 22; Matt 10:29-31; Ps 116:15; Acts 2:24; 1 Cor 15:54-57; Heb 2:15; Rom 8:38-39)

Chapter 6—Sufferings in Ministry | 62

This chapter focuses on major sufferings that I've been through that are correlated with my life in the ministry. These are sufferings that have all come during my ten years as a missionary in China. These include:

1 Getting Kicked Out of My College in Eastern China (Rom 8:28)

2 Rejection by IMB

3 Suffering in Ministry Leadership (Num 11:14)

4 I Have Been Constantly on the Move (2 Cor 11:26)

CONTENTS

Chapter 7—Other Sufferings | 71

> This chapter covers some other very unique major trials in my life. These include:
>
> 1. Being Egyptian Revolution Witnesses in 2011 (Ps 62:2)
> 2. Suffering through Intense Anxiety in Seminary (2 Cor 1:3–6, 9)
> 3. Suffering through Miscarriage at Five Months Pregnant
> 4. Suffering When Things Seem Well

Chapter 8—Conclusion | 86

> 1. Remembering God's Deliverances and Miracles in Our Lives from the Past (Ps 77:10–12)
> 2. How Jeremiah Had Hope in the Darkest of Times (Lam 3:19–20, 21–26)

Section I

Biblical Principles About Suffering

1

What's This Book About?

WHEN I WAS A sophomore in college I studied abroad in England for the whole school year. It was sometime during that year that I first truly became a Christian, though I'm not exactly sure on the precise date. But during the spring semester and the summer, some friends and I had a couple months to backpack around Europe. We bought the Eurail Pass and just rode trains all around most of Western Europe, Scandinavia, the United Kingdom, and some of Eastern Europe. We stayed at hostels in each place, sleeping sometimes in beds with over a hundred beds in one huge room. We saw lots of museums and cathedrals, and played much hacky sack, as well as eating many things like gyros, gelato, and peanut butter sandwiches. It was quite an adventure and all of us had grown out scraggly beards and hair to properly play the backpacker role.

It was during the first month of traveling, as I was with a group of five Americans traveling together, that I was heavily influenced by my friend whom everyone called "Scoop." I'd known Scoop from college in Oklahoma, though not as great friends at the time. He was a couple years older than me and he had wisdom way beyond his years. He proposed that we should have a weekly Bible study in the trains as we travelled from city to city around Europe. And we were okay to do that, with all of us at least coming from some kind of church background. Plus, as Scoop was the oldest in our traveling group, none were about to oppose him.

In a few cities I was fortunate enough to be able to stay alone with Scoop in a hostel room and get to chat with him more. I could ask him many more questions about God. He was able to answer many of my hard questions. He answered questions with answers

SECTION I: BIBLICAL PRINCIPLES ABOUT SUFFERING

that actually made sense and were based on the Scriptures. I shared with him about some hardships in my life, particularly about how my mom was at that time in a nursing home with a genetic and incurable neurological disease. I was telling him about the many reasons why I thought that my life stunk at that time. And I still remember very clearly Scoop's response to me.

I thought he would show some sympathy to me, but instead he said, "Don't you think God is in control, even over disease and death?" I couldn't believe that he'd respond in such a way! I was hoping that he'd just pour more fuel to my pity party. But instead he really flipped me on my head with his response. Could what Scoop said actually be true? Could God truly be in control, even over disease and death? I didn't understand God to be very relevant to my personal life at that time. God was just relevant when I'd go to church on Sundays. But he was not relevant to the rest of my life, especially the very hard things. But Scoop was saying something different. He was saying that God was not only relevant in my life, but he was in complete control over each hair on my head and each sparrow in the sky.

Through that conversation with Scoop in the hostel in Barcelona, the Lord sparked something in me. There was a seed that was planted in my heart about God's sovereignty over all things. I really started to think about whether this crazy Scoop guy could actually be right. Over the next couple years of college, I started reading much more of the Bible. I read some great classics on God's sovereignty: *Trusting God* by Jerry Bridges, and *Pleasures of God* by John Piper. These books taught me even more about the extent of God's sovereignty. And since then, the Lord has taught me much more about God's sovereignty over all things, including his sovereignty in our sufferings.

Since then, I've had various trials and have had to be repeatedly reminded personally through the fires of hardships. When the times are good, we don't think about such things. But when times are bad, we must cry out to the Lord and say, "Why?!" And then we must again remind ourselves about God's character and what his Word teaches to us about his sovereignty in all things, even in our sufferings. This book, *In the Fiery Furnace of Suffering*, is a biblical and personal reflection on Christian suffering. It explores themes like suffering, death, and the sovereignty of God, first through biblical exposition and then through personal reflection. The first half of the book explores what the Bible says on matters like the origins of suffering, how to suffer well, and how God wants to use our sufferings. The second half of the book includes accounts of my own personal sufferings.

This book is not simply about the doctrines of death, suffering, or the sovereignty of God, but about these doctrines dealt with on a personal level, as related through accounts of my own sufferings. The Lord has granted me lots of experience in suffering, and through those experiences I've had to constantly be reminded of what the Bible says about suffering. These are not simply ideas in my head. Rather, they've been burned onto my heart through the blazing furnace of adversity and pain. I want to make these things known to the readers of this book, and hope it may encourage the reader to have a better picture of what the Bible as a whole—Old Testament and New Testament—says about suffering, as well as how my unique experiences in suffering are related to the Bible. Hopefully readers will be able to relate to some aspects of my own sufferings. And they definitely as Christians should be pushed to consider God's sovereignty in suffering, and the many other dynamics of suffering from a biblical perspective. And hopefully they can apply these biblical ideas to their past, present, or future sufferings.

2

Origin of Suffering

PEOPLE MAY THINK THAT our sufferings only come from Satan and that God completely has no part in them. Some think that God only gives "good" things to us, and Satan is responsible for all things in our lives that are deemed as "bad." Many people in churches also think that any kind of suffering or ailment is from Satan and must be cast out by all means. However, this is not the correct understanding of the origin of our sufferings that we see in the Bible. The book of Ecclesiastes says, "Consider what God has done. Who can straighten what he has made crooked? When times are good, be happy. But when times are bad, consider: God has made the one as well as the other" (Eccl 7:13–14). Similarly, the Lord elsewhere says, "Who can speak and have it happen if the Lord has not decreed it? Is it not from the mouth of the Most High that both calamities and good things come?" (Lam 3:37–38) Both of these Scriptures are referring to the reality that it is from the mouth of the Most High that both good and bad things come.

The same idea is seen in the story of Job and God's interpretation of Job's reaction to his great loss of family and possessions and health. Job's response to his great affliction was, "The Lord gave and the Lord has taken away; may the name of the Lord be praised" (Job 1:21). And God's response to Job's reaction is, "In all this, Job did not sin by charging God with wrongdoing" (Job 1:22). The next chapter, when Job is afflicted with sores and his wife yells at Job, Job responds, "Shall we accept good from God, and not trouble?" And again God's conclusion on Job's response is, "In all this, Job did not sin in what he said" (Job 2:10). Job sees that God is sovereign over the good and the bad in his life. Job knows that it truly is the Lord who gives and takes away. And thus, Job is blameless in having such an understanding of God during Job's time of family and personal crisis.

What all these authors are saying is that good times are from God. And bad times are also from God. All of them are from God. It is not as though the bad times happen to us when God is not paying attention. These verses are not saying that good things come from God and bad things come from Satan. Certainly Satan is a real accuser and afflicter of God's people. But the Bible teaches us quite clearly that Satan does nothing that is beyond God's hand to stop, and that God is completely sovereign over all things in the universe, including the fiery trials that may come our way.

Job's Sufferings

We can see a great example of God's sovereignty over suffering by looking at the story of Job in the Old Testament. God allowed Satan to inflict great afflictions on Job and everything he had, even with physical ailments. If God allowed Satan to afflict Job in such awful ways, what was God's purpose in Job's afflictions? Was God just cruel and heartless, and just enjoyed seeing people be tortured? No, of course that was not the case.

God did not directly test Job, as it was not God who directly afflicted Job, but God did use Satan's afflicting of Job to test the depth of Job's faith in him. As Satan accurately states, it is easy to trust in God when everything is going your way and you have everything you could ever dream to have (Job 1:10). Anyone can praise God in such a state of wealth and success. It is another thing when you have nothing and you are still able to fully praise the Lord (Job 1:11). Once Job was afflicted, certainly he did have many doubts and grumblings against God, which is only natural when going through great affliction. But through the process, Job was able to grow in his faith and knowledge of God. God is most glorified through a suffering saint like Job being able to continue to sing God's praises through and after the storms blow.

SECTION I: BIBLICAL PRINCIPLES ABOUT SUFFERING

God's very simple design for our afflictions is that, if we are not believers in the first place, through being brought completely low before the Lord through our sufferings we may come to true knowledge of the one true God. And if we are already believers, God desires that the afflictions that come our way may be used to strengthen our faith and trust in him.

As mentioned earlier, Peter talks about this very same idea in the New Testament. Peter writes that the trials that come our way may be for the purpose that "our faith—of greater worth than gold, which perishes even though refined by fire—may be proved genuine and may result in praise, glory and honor when Jesus Christ is revealed" (1 Pet 1:7). What a sweet verse this is! Peter essentially is summing up what Job learned through his sufferings: though painful and confusing at the time, the Lord desires to use those sufferings in order that we may bring more glory to him by the purification and sanctification of our faith.

Lord, You Have Assigned Me My Portion and My Cup

We can see another awesome example in Psalm 16 about God's sovereignty over all aspects of our lives. In that chapter, David is talking about the Lord's faithfulness to him. David says things like how the Lord is "his refuge" (v. 1) and how the Lord "will not abandon him to the grave" (v. 10). In the middle of this sweet chapter about God's faithfulness are a couple verses about God's amazing sovereignty and goodness to us. David writes, "Lord you have assigned me my portion and my cup. You have made my lot secure . . . Surely I have a delightful inheritance" (v. 5–6). This is a simple but profound truth. The Lord has assigned our lot in life to us.

We read in a later psalm about how God already knows everything that will happen to us, that "all of our days are written in his book before one of them comes to be" (Ps 139:16). So the Lord not only knows everything that will come to pass, but he actively assigns it. And he has given each of us the lot that he knows results in his greatest glory. In the chapter right before this David writes,

"The Lord will fulfill his purpose for me . . . Do not abandon the works of your hands" (Ps 138:8). God has a particular purpose for his people. And it's impossible to know exactly why God does certain things. But we can know with certainty that all things that come to pass are for the magnification of God's own glory.

And part of the truth in the Scriptures about the lot that the Lord has given us is that God is also sovereign over things in our lives. There are many examples of this in the Scriptures. I'll mention a few. God says, "I form the light and create darkness. I bring prosperity and create disaster. I the Lord do all these things" (Isa 45:7). So the Lord brings both prosperity and disaster. He is sovereign over it all. And in Exodus 4:11 God says, "Who gave man his mouth? Who makes him deaf or mute? Who gives him sight or makes him blind? Is it not I, the Lord?" So in each of these examples we see how the Lord brings both good things and bad things alike. It would be wrong for us to say that all good things are from the Lord and all bad things are from Satan or someone else. But even to think about what is "good" or "bad" is not for our own judgment.

What we may think of something that is very "bad," like losing our job or having some serious physical affliction, may be exactly something that God is using to purify our faith and make us rely even more on him. Or maybe he is using our circumstances to draw someone else closer to him. There are just too many things going on within any given moment around the whole universe. We can only understand how things affect us. But we have no idea about how and what God uses to affect people around the globe. Our understanding of God's redemption plan and everything God does for that plan is so poor and limited.

These are just a few examples that reveal God's sovereignty over all things that happen in the universe. I could've listed many others. But the Lord is sovereign over the lot in our life. We have received the lot that the Lord has given to us. So we can have some assurance in our sufferings that the Lord is using them for our own good. And he is not only sovereign, but he is good and he is wise. If he is infinitely wise, good, and sovereign, then we can trust in his goodness to us even when we think there is nothing possibly good that could come from our circumstances. And in such situations, he knows what is good for us.

Some Sufferings Are from the Enemy

Peter writes to the church leaders specifically in 1 Peter 5 to be aware of the devil's presence. He writes, "Be self-controlled and alert. Your enemy the devil prowls around like a roaring lion looking for someone to devour" (5:8). So Peter is warning the church leaders to be aware of the reality of spiritual warfare around them. Though they cannot physically see the enemy lurking, the devil is prowling around like a roaring lion waiting to devour them. If they are not aware and conscious of this reality, they will be swallowed whole and defeated.

And then Peter, after encouraging the brothers to resist the enemy prowling around like a roaring lion, writes about the Lord's will in such sufferings, even those that come from the devil. Peter writes, "And the God of all grace, who called you to his eternal glory in Christ, after you have a suffered a little while, will himself restore you and make you strong, firm and steadfast" (5:10). So in this situation, it is not the devil that has the last word. It is God, who uses this suffering to strengthen the faith and steadfastness of his children.

But when the devil aims to devour us like a roaring lion, he is not limitless in what he can do to us. Just like in the story of Job, God was over the devil's activity and the devil could attack Job no more than what God allowed him to do. So it is not as though the devil destroyed Job's life and then God had to frantically pick up the broken pieces of Job's life. Rather, the Lord's hand is over all of it, though he was not the one who directly attacked Job. The Lord's will in Job's affliction is that the Lord will restore him after his sufferings and make him strong, firm, and steadfast.

We see this same concept in Luke 22 when Jesus is telling Simon Peter about how he will end up betraying Jesus. Right before this, Jesus mentions to Simon Peter that Satan wants to completely pulverize and destroy Simon. Jesus says, "Simon, Simon, Satan has asked to sift you as wheat" (v. 31). So Jesus is essentially telling Simon that Satan is prowling around like a roaring lion, ready to attack. Satan wants to "sift him as wheat," which means to completely toss him around and grind him up like a garbage disposal. Jesus is correct, of course, because right after this Simon does fall into Satan's trap and deny Jesus three times.

Though Simon is completely responsible and guilty in his heart-wrenching backstabbing of his best friend and the Lord of the universe, Simon is not the only one responsible for this betrayal of Jesus. Satan is also quite active in filling Simon's heart with fears and thoughts of self-preservation, to such an extent that Simon would betray the very man that just moments earlier he had said he would die for without hesitation.

That being said, after Jesus tells Simon Peter that Satan wants to sift him as wheat, Jesus does not give up on the failure of the man Simon altogether. No, though Satan thinks he is victorious over Simon Peter's soul, what Satan doesn't know is that Simon Peter's soul is not in Satan's hands, but rather in Christ Jesus' hands. Jesus says, "I have prayed for you Simon, that your faith may not fail" (Luke 22:32). So Jesus, the great high priest, the bridge connecting us and God, tells Simon that he is interceding on Simon's behalf. He prays with earnestness that despite the attacks from Satan, Simon's faith will prevail. Jesus prays Simon may not quit serving his Savior. That is Jesus' prayer for him.

And Jesus closes with sweet words to Simon Peter: "When you have turned back, strengthen your brothers" (v. 32). So Jesus is not done with Simon Peter. Though Simon is moments away from falling flat on his face in complete failure, Jesus is not done with him. He hasn't given up on him. He knows that Simon Peter will be one of the main leaders of the early church for many decades, serving his King Jesus resolutely and fearlessly. Satan has not had the last word with Simon Peter. Rather, just like in the story with Job, God uses sufferings instigated by Satan in order to make his children fearless and zealous ambassadors of his gospel. If anything, Simon forever after this testified with power about

SECTION I: BIBLICAL PRINCIPLES ABOUT SUFFERING

his Savior's mercy and love on him even in the midst of this very shameful betrayal.

Paul elsewhere writes some good stuff to Christians in Ephesus about the reality of the enemy, that we are to put on the armor of God to fight against the devil. Paul writes that what we can see with our eyes is not all that exists in this universe. In fact, there's a whole spiritual realm that we cannot see at all, much of which is desiring to war with God and go to all costs to crush his people. Paul writes, "Our struggle is not against flesh and blood, but against the rulers, against the authorities, against the powers of this dark world and against the spiritual forces of evil in the heavenly realms" (Eph 6:12).

In the Old Testament we can see a good picture of the work of enemies against God's people. In the book of Nehemiah, many of the Jews had just returned to Jerusalem after being exiled to Babylon. Nehemiah was trying to gather them together to rebuild the temple. The Jews were met with much opposition, though. Nehemiah 4:10–16 talks about how the strength of the laborers is giving out (v. 10). They're exhausted. The enemy is lurking and ready to kill the Israelites (v. 11).

The enemy desires that God's people and their service to God may both be destroyed. The Jews recognize that they are being attacked (v. 12). They cry out in distress. Nehemiah then decides to post people with their families behind the lowest and weakest parts of the wall (v. 13). They can work together to help keep the wall from falling. They stand vigilantly, with their swords, spears, and bows in hand. When we are being attacked, we must use the armor of God: the belt of truth, the breastplate of righteousness, feet fitted with the readiness that comes from the gospel of peace, the shield of faith, the helmet of salvation, and the sword of the Spirit (Eph 6:10–20). This is how we help keep the wall from crushing in on us from the constant pressure and onslaught from the enemy.

Next Nehemiah tries to rally the troops and unite all the Israelites against their enemy (v. 14). Rather than being terrified about the lurking enemy, the Israelites are to remember the Lord. He is great and awesome. All of them are fighting together for a common cause, which is the glory of God. In the same way, we are to fight for the spiritual welfare of those closest to us. We're all in the fight together. We're on the same side. We are all working together for the common cause of the spread of the fame of our King's name to all corners of the earth.

Once the Israelites recognized the enemy's presence and power and turned to the Lord, they then returned to the work (v. 15). There is still a temple to be built. When we are attacked by enemies, we also must return to the work in serving God. The very thing that our enemies want us to do is to stop serving God. So if we stop in what we are doing, then we are actually doing exactly what the enemy wants us to do. So we must put our head down and keep moving forward in the work.

At the end of this story, Nehemiah split up the men in their work. Half would do the work, while the other half would stand in guard with their spears, shields, bows, and armor (v. 16). Certainly we can see the need to cover each other's back in serving God. It is not intended that we do everything on our own and only rely on ourselves. Also, though we may not stand guard with battle weapons like the Israelites did, we still are called to have the armor of God on.

In Ephesians 6 Paul concludes the armor of God section by writing about how we are to help believers who are being attacked by the enemy. We stand guard protecting our brothers and sisters by "being alert and always keeping on praying for all the saints" (Eph 6:18). Like in the story of Nehemiah, we carry a big bulk of the weight of the work by equipping ourselves with the armor of God and praying for the people of God. We pray for their protection from the enemies. This is the primary way that we can stand guard and intercede for the saints and their service to God as they face constant threats from opposition by the spiritual forces of evil surrounding them.

SECTION I: BIBLICAL PRINCIPLES ABOUT SUFFERING

Some Sufferings Are a Result of Our Own Sin

A common theme throughout the Bible is the idea that if we walk with God, we will be blessed by God. If we stray from God and walk in sin, then we will be punished by God. This idea goes back to the beginning of the Bible, and is seen clearly in Leviticus 26. God lists many blessings that the Israelites will receive if they obey (i.e., "I will send rain in season, and the ground will yield its crops . . . There will be peace in the land . . . You will defeat your enemies . . . You will increase in numbers . . . I will dwell with you"). These blessings are so great that it is a wonder how the Israelites struggled so hard to obey God.

But, according to Leviticus 26, if the Israelites disobeyed they would be heavily punished by the Lord (i.e., "I will bring you sudden terror, wasting diseases and fever . . . You will be defeated by your enemies . . . Your soil will not yield its crops . . . I will send a plague among you . . . I will scatter you among the nations"). There is such a discrepancy between the blessings received through obedience and the curses that result from disobedience, it is unbelievable that the Israelites could have such hardened hearts to persist in disobedience even after such stern warnings from God.

An example of God giving us sufferings as a result of our sin is in 2 Samuel 12. Nathan confronts King David about how David has sinned against God. David is guilty of adultery with Bathsheba, and also guilty of murdering Bathsheba's husband, Uriah. Nathan tells David about his awful sin (v. 7), and then David's heart is convicted of his sin and he cries out to the Lord for mercy, "I have sinned against the Lord" (v. 13). Nathan's response to David is that the Lord "has taken away [his] sin" (v. 14). But, as a result of David's sin, "the son born to him will die" (v. 14). So David pleads to the Lord for forgiveness of his heinous sins. The Lord responds that David's sins have been forgiven of him. In the Lord's eyes, David's slate is considered wiped clean, and his sins have "been made white as snow" (Isa 1:18).

However, God's message to David is not that it is though David had never sinned in the first place. No, unfortunately for David, he cannot erase what he has done. He cannot push the rewind button and have another try to do better. Rather, what is done is done. The damage of David's sins against Uriah, Bathsheba, David's wife, against the baby, and against others cannot be forgotten altogether.

This is why the Lord says to David that because of David's sin, his newborn son will die. And the baby did indeed die (v. 19). When we sin, God's punishment to us is not usually that a loved one will die as a result of our sin. But, at the same time, when we sin, there are always longer-term consequences. It could be that when we fall into sin, it makes it easier for us to fall into the same sins again down the road. It could be that we have angered loved ones around us and they have lost some kind of trust in us. Or we have sinned against those in our church. It could be that we looked at pornography habitually for many years and, because of this, our minds will forever continue to have flashbacks of those pornographic images. Like in the story of David and his sin with Bathsheba, there are real consequences that ensue when we sin. Our slate with God may be "wiped clean" when we cry out for his forgiveness. But we still can continue to suffer long afterwards as a result of our sin. It is not in all regards literally as though we had never sinned at all in the first place, as much as we may want it to be that way.

3

How to Suffer Well

Is it possible to suffer in a biblical manner when we're in the midst of sufferings? What exactly would suffering in a biblical manner entail? Certainly our natural reaction when going through sufferings is to feel angry at God or to feel self-pity. We feel like we've been cursed for some reason. Our lives were going smooth until God messed everything up by sending these undesirable things into our lives. This is our natural way to respond to sufferings, but this is not the biblical way. So what exactly does the Bible say about what mindset we are to have while we are experiencing a fiery trial? We want to respond in a way that brings glory to God. And thankfully the Scriptures tell us what that involves.

Remember God Delivers His People through Fiery Trials

Something that is a common theme throughout the Bible is the reality that God carries his people through the hardest trials and delivers them. An example of this is God delivering the boy David from the hand of the God-hating giant Goliath in 1 Samuel 17. Another example is Peter being delivered from prison by an angel of God (Acts 12). God is a God who delivers his people. These are just a couple of examples of God delivering his people in the Bible.

A great story in the Old Testament about God delivering his people in the most desperate situation can be seen in the story of God parting the Red Sea through Moses (Exod 14). Right before the Lord brought the Israelites through the Red Sea, the Israelites' situation looked incredibly bleak. It seemed as though Pharaoh and the Egyptians in their chariots were soon to overtake the Israelites and kill them. The Egyptians had overtaken the Israelites and the Israelites were trapped. Everyone panicked and cried out to Moses (v. 9).

And Moses responded to the people, "Do not be afraid. Stand firm and you will see the deliverance the Lord will bring for you today . . . The Lord will fight for you. You need only to be still" (v. 14–15). And then the Lord brought a miraculous deliverance to the Egyptians by sending a pillar of cloud between the two armies (v. 19). And then the larger miracle from God was sending a wind that turned the sea into dry land (v. 21). The Israelites crossed the Red Sea by walking right through the middle of it (v. 22). The Egyptians continued their pursuit, and were washed away when God let the sea come back down upon them once the Israelites had safely crossed (v. 28). This story gives us a great picture of God's love for his people. And it also shows us that he is a God who is a deliverer in our times of greatest need.

Similarly, when we are going through the hardest of trials, just like the situation of Moses and the Israelites when they realized they were trapped by the Egyptians and were doomed to die, we must call on the Lord to deliver us and carry us through those trials. And certainly Moses' words to the Israelites in Exodus 14:14–15 are a great model for us to follow when we are in great despair and fear: "Do not be afraid. Stand firm and you will see the deliverance the Lord will bring you today. The Lord will fight for you. You need only to be still." We should not fear death or anything. We shall stand firm and wait for the Lord to deliver us. He will fight for us, and we just need to be quiet and still before him. This story clearly shows the character of God as being the one who is the Great Deliverer.

The point of this story about God parting the Red Sea through Moses' hand to deliver the Israelites out of Egypt is not to say that in any similar situation we can expect the same result. Certainly when we cry out to the Lord to deliver us from those who want to persecute or kill us, there is no guarantee that the Lord will deliver us and keep us safe and out of harm's way. If we are in an intense

SECTION I: BIBLICAL PRINCIPLES ABOUT SUFFERING

trial and cry out to the Lord to deliver us from that trial, God does not promise that he will end the trial and make our lives pain free. But we are promised by God that, even in death, "nothing will separate us from the love of God that is in Christ Jesus our Lord" (Rom 8:38–39).

Isaiah 43:1–3 gives a great look at how the Lord carries his people through the hardest trials. God says, "Fear not, for I have redeemed you. I have called you by name; you are mine" (v. 1). So God declares that the Israelites should not be afraid. God has called and redeemed them. And God continues, "When you pass through the waters I will be with you ... When you walk through the fire you will not be burned" (v. 2). Maybe the Lord's reference here to "passing through the waters" is related to the Lord bringing them out of Egypt by parting the Red Sea and bringing the Israelites through to safety. Maybe the Lord is referring to other instances of him bringing the Israelites safely through rivers or seas. And the reference to "walking through the fire and not being burned" must be looking at an instance of God's deliverance of the Israelites.

The main point is that the Lord has carried the Israelites through the hardest of times. They can pass through the waters and come out safely to the other end. They can walk though a fire and not be burned. The Lord protects and carries his people through the fiery trials that they face. An example of God literally carrying his people through a fire and not being burned is in Daniel 3. Nebuchadnezzar arrests Shadrach, Meshach, and Abednego because they refuse to bow down and worship his golden statue. Nebuchadnezzar threatens them with death by fire if they continue to rebel against him. And their response to him is, "If we are thrown into the blazing furnace, the God we serve is able to save us from it, and he will rescue us from your hand, O king" (Dan 3:17).

They do not budge at Nebuchadnezzar's threats, even to the risk of their own lives. They believe that God can rescue them from the king's hand. They believe that even if they are thrown into the blazing fire, God will deliver them. Though Nebuchadnezzar turned up the heat of the furnace to seven times hotter than normal (3:19), the three men survive in the fire (v. 26). God's will was not to save them out of the fire, necessarily, but to save them through the fire. This story is another example of how God delivers his people in the most treacherous and terrifying of circumstances. Like with the story of the three men in the fire, God similarly may not want to save us out of the fire of our trials, but to leave us in the fire and save us and purify us going through the hottest flames of the fire.

Another place in the Old Testament that has a similar idea of God's deliverance in trials is found in Psalm 124:1, 4–5. David writes, "If the Lord had not been on our side . . . the flood would have engulfed us . . . [and] the raging waters would have swept us away." In other words, the Lord's presence by the Israelites' side is key to their survival. If the Lord had not been present when the flood came, the waves would have overwhelmed and completely covered them. If the Lord had not been there when the raging waters came, the Israelites would have been swept away and never to be seen again. But, the Lord was there with them at their side. Because of that, the Israelites were still standing. When we feel entirely overwhelmed by a particular trial in our lives, and feel like we are completely falling apart and losing our minds, may we trust in the Lord to carry us through the "raging waters."

An example from the New Testament of God delivering his people through fiery trials is in Hebrews 10 and 11. The end of Hebrews 10 mentions those standing firm in their faith amidst much opposition (10:32). They joyfully accepted the stealing of their property because they knew they had an eternal inheritance in heaven (10:34). They are called to persevere in their faith (10:36), and they are not to shrink back in fear but to believe and be saved (10:39). Then Hebrews 11 gives many examples of those from the past who have persevered in the faith and have not shrank back in fear. This list includes people like Abraham, Jacob, Moses, Rahab, and David. The Lord helped some of these people of faith "conquer kingdoms, shut the mouths of lions, quench the fury of the flames, and escape the edge of the sword" (11:33–34). The Lord even helped pull people through such awful trials as being tortured,

SECTION I: BIBLICAL PRINCIPLES ABOUT SUFFERING

being flogged, being chained in prison, being stoned, being sawed in two, and being put to death by the sword (11:35–37).

How does the Lord carry his people through such trials? The beautiful beginning of Hebrews 12 that perfectly follows the extensive list of people of faith that God carried through trials is this: "Let us run with perseverance the race marked out for us. Let us fix our eyes on Jesus, the author and perfecter of our faith, who for the joy set before him endured the cross, scorning its shame, and sat down at the right hand of the throne of God" (12:1–2). And the next verse shows us how fixing our eyes on Jesus will help us persevere through trials: "Consider him who endured such opposition from sinful men, so that you will not grow weary and lose heart" (12:3).

Following this long list of people of faith, the writer of Hebrews tells us how they persevered through the most difficult of trials, and how we can do the same. Just like those people of faith did, we are to fix our eyes on Jesus and cling to him. And we are to not only consider his shame and humiliation on the cross, and his victory through his resurrection. But we are to also think about those who opposed Jesus even to the point of murdering him. Because of this example, we are also to—by fixing our eyes on Christ—endure spiritual and worldly opposition we face in this world. And the Lord will carry us through even the worst and most overwhelming and impossible-to-handle trials we can imagine.

Another example of God delivering his people in the New Testament is in 2 Timothy 4:17–18. Paul writes, "I was delivered from the lion's mouth. The Lord will rescue me from evil attack and will bring me safely to his heavenly kingdom." Paul is stating that God has delivered him from the gravest of dangers. And Paul has confidence that God will continue to deliver him from any trials that come upon him.

Paul's confidence of the Lord's continued deliverance in his life based on the Lord's past deliverances in his life is quite similar to David's words about how God will provide for him against Goliath. David says, "The Lord who delivered me from the paw of the lion and the paw of the bear will deliver me from the hand of this

Philistine" (1 Sam 17:37). David is saying that God has delivered him from the paw of the lion and the paw of the bear. Why would there be any reason to think that God will not deliver him from the hand of Goliath? The Lord has brought David through intense life-threatening trials, and the Lord will continue to do so. David has a sense of confidence, not in his own strength in combat, but in the Lord's power to deliver him time and time again.

Do Not Be Surprised at the Painful Trial You Are Suffering

In the book of 1 Peter, the author Peter gives a great section about suffering at the end of chapter 4 (vv. 12–19). He talks about what our attitudes should be like as we go through suffering. The very beginning of this section is quite a profound statement: "Do not be surprised at the painful trial you are suffering, as though something strange were happening to you" (v. 12). I think even as believers when we first begin to go through a period of suffering, we naturally feel surprised that the Lord would put such trials in our path. The most typical question in such times is to ask God, "Why me?!" We enjoy living a smooth and comfortable carefree life. That is much more enjoyable for us than to hit any bumps on the road.

Often when a trial is upon us, we may want to say to God, "Are you kidding me?!" Our lives our smooth, and we want to blame God for disrupting our peaceful existence. Maybe a thought in our minds is that our lives would be much better if God weren't messing everything up. But Peter tells us what our appropriate initial reaction to suffering should be. We should not be surprised at those sufferings. We should not think that something strange is happening to us. On the other hand, sufferings are an inevitable and necessary part of following Christ. If we are going through trials as a believer, nothing even the least bit strange is happening to us. We are to accept this as a normal part of our Christian life, just like reading the Bible, praying, or diving into our church life.

So what should our reaction to sufferings be? Well, Peter answers that well in the next verse: "Rejoice that you participate in the sufferings of Christ, so that you may be overjoyed when his glory is revealed" (1 Pet 4:13). So our first reaction to sufferings should not be to feel surprised or to blame God and think that something strange is happening to us. This is a natural response for us to have, but it is not the response that is most glorifying to God. Rather, the proper response is to recognize that sufferings are a necessary part of being a Christian, and we are to rejoice that we can participate in the sufferings of Christ. And in those sufferings, we can even more yearn for Christ's return and his glory to be revealed.

This is similar to Jesus' words: "In this world you will have trouble. But take heart! I have overcome the world" (John 16:33). Jesus tells us the troubles are coming. Like with the words of Peter, Jesus tells us that suffering is inevitable and will certainly come. There is no avoiding it. But when those sufferings come we are to be strengthened, and remember that Christ has overcome the world. Like with Peter writing about in our sufferings to rejoice in the future glory of Christ that will be revealed, so also Jesus tells us that in the midst of our sufferings we should remember that Jesus has defeated death and Satan and we will be with him for eternity. This focus on the eternal inheritance is what will carry us through the fire.

We Must Go through Many Hardships to Enter the Kingdom of God

In a similar manner, we are told in the Scriptures to expect sufferings in our lives. We can see one example of this in a story about Paul and his traveling companions in Acts 14:21–25. Paul and some others are traveling back to the cities that they've already served in before, encouraging the new believers in their faith and urging them towards persevering in the faith. Paul has ministered in these cities before. He loves these people deeply. He may not have seen them for a while, and certainly he has no idea when he will see them again after that. So we can imagine that Paul will communicate the most important things to these sweet brothers and sisters, that they may flourish and reproduce in their faith long after Paul has left.

And what is the message that Paul emphasizes to them? We see his emphasis in the one quoted sentence that Luke wrote down in this account: "We must go through many hardships to enter the kingdom of God" (v. 22). Certainly I'm sure that Paul said many other things to these believers during their time together. We don't know exactly what they talked about. But this one quoted sentence is what Luke chose to write down. So it must be important. The most important thing that Paul can say to these young believers to prepare them for a life of faithfulness is that they must go through many hardships to enter the kingdom of God.

So if we are to live a life devoted to the Lord, we must expect that we must go through many trials to enter the kingdom of God. This is not an optional part of being a Christian. We cannot choose devotion to Christ and an easy life with no hardships. Rather, the two go hand in hand. If we are to live a life devoted to Christ, then sufferings will necessarily come with it.

But oh, how worthwhile a faithful devotion to Christ is! As Paul writes in Romans 8:18, "I consider that our present sufferings are not worth comparing with the glory that will be revealed in me." And similarly in 2 Corinthinas 4:17, "Our light and momentary troubles are achieving for us an eternal glory that far outweighs them all." So, though sufferings in our lives are real and completely painful, the glory that awaits a persevered saint is infinitely more intense and grand than any pain we've experienced on this earth. On that day, we will not have even a thought about the trials we've experienced in our lives. That day when we meet Christ will be too glorious! We will be clothed in our heavenly tents, our glorified bodies. And we will be with Christ forever.

Rejoice in Your Sufferings

It is one thing to not be surprised when we face sufferings, or to understand that going through trials is part of being a believer. We can even think about the English expression that "every cloud

SECTION I: BIBLICAL PRINCIPLES ABOUT SUFFERING

has its silver lining." But the Bible takes this idea a step further. The Bible says we are to rejoice in our sufferings. We are not only to endure through sufferings, but we are to rejoice in them. How can this be possible? Wouldn't it make more sense if the Bible told us we should rejoice anytime we are not suffering? Why would anyone rejoice in the midst of sufferings?

James writes that we are to "consider it pure joy when we face trials of many kinds, because we know that the testing of our faith develops perseverance" (Jas 1:2–3). We can imagine that we have some kind of great (or even small) physical affliction or trial of some kind. For myself, even if I have a minor crick in my neck for one day I can get incredibly irritable and cranky. And that's just for a very tiny physical affliction. In such moments, is it even in my mind to praise God for it? No, mostly I'm grumbling to God about how he could inconvenience my life at that moment so much by giving me a neck crick.

So it's one thing to tolerate suffering and not get too upset about it. We can sometimes bite our tongues to keep us from verbally complaining and grumbling in self-pity. But it's a completely different thing to consider affliction as a great joy. But that's exactly what God wants us to do. And the reason we are to consider it pure joy when we go through sufferings is because we recognize that the Lord is sovereign over those sufferings. He wants to purify our faith that it may be stronger. If we truly understand the final end that God has in sight for us in our sufferings, then we can consider them pure joy because we know they are for our ultimate best interest.

Paul writes about delighting in his sufferings at the end of the section about the thorn in his flesh: "For Christ's sake, I delight in weaknesses, in insults, in hardships, in persecutions, in difficulties. For when I am weak, then I am strong" (2 Cor 12:10). Paul is expressing how he does not simply try to survive his hardships, but he delights in them. He recognizes that through the power of Christ within him, when Paul is weak, then he is strong.

Another similar verse is in Romans 5:3–5. Paul writes, "We also rejoice in our sufferings, because we know that suffering produces perseverance; perseverance, character; and character, hope. And hope does not disappoint us." These verses are very similar to what James was saying in his letter about considering it pure joy when we face sufferings, because we know that through such trials God is developing perseverance in us.

Firstly, Paul writes that we are to rejoice in our sufferings. Why on earth are we to rejoice in our sufferings? Well, we see God's divine purpose in the result of our sufferings, namely, that through them God will build perseverance in us. And through our growth in perseverance in faith, God will build our character. And through our development of godly character, God will cultivate in us more hope. While suffering, often it is quite difficult to have any hope in anything, much less in God. But what Paul is writing is that one thing God uses our sufferings for is to actually increase our hope in him, rather than decreasing it. This may seem impossible, but that's exactly what Paul is writing here.

Sharing in Christ's Sufferings

Paul thought it important that he strive to share in the sufferings of Christ. This was something that Paul rejoiced in and sought after. Why was this so important for Paul? What can we learn about as far as how we can have a biblical mindset when we face sufferings? An example of Paul mentioning sharing in Christ's sufferings is Romans 8:17, where Paul writes that if we are children of God, we are coheirs with Christ if we "share in Christ's sufferings in order that we may also share in his glory." So for Paul when we share in Christ's sufferings we also share in Christ's glory. When we suffer for Christ, we feel an intimacy with Christ. Just as Christ suffered through his arrest and crucifixion, we can share with him that suffering when we go through trials of various kinds.

This is why Paul writes elsewhere, "It has been granted to you on behalf of Christ not only believe to on him, but also to suffer for him" (Phil 1:29). So Paul sees that we as Christians are called to suffer. Later in Philippians Paul writes, "I want to know Christ and the power of his resurrection and the fellowship of sharing in his sufferings, becoming like him in his death, and so to attain to the resurrection from the dead" (3:10–11). When we suffer for Christ, we feel a tight bond with him.

Sharing in Christ's sufferings is not simply a duty, but it should also be a type of honor for us. Peter writes that we are to rejoice that we "participate in the sufferings of Christ, so that we may be overjoyed when his glory is revealed" (1 Pet 4:13). We are to rejoice that we share in Christ's sufferings. We can see this displayed at the end of Acts 5 when the apostles were flogged and ordered not to speak anymore in the name of Jesus. And the response of the apostles after their flogging was, "the apostles left the Sanhedrin, rejoicing because they had been counted worthy of suffering disgrace for the Name" (Acts 5:41).

How does our shared sufferings with Christ bring glory to him? The apostles rejoiced because they suffered for the name of Jesus. When we suffer for Jesus' name, we are to rejoice. We can go through trials, and point all those around us towards Christ as we go through those trials. We can be a witness to the world of how Christ gave us strength and perseverance through the toughest of times. When this happens, Christ is glorified and his name is raised high. In such times, the glory is not to us but to him.

Consider How Temporary Our Life Is

In putting God at the center of our lives in the midst of suffering, we must consider how temporary our life on earth is. As David writes, "Show me, O Lord, my life's end and the number of my days. Let me know how fleeting is my life" (Ps 39:4). The reason this psalm jumps out at me is that David is thinking much differently than we as humans naturally think. As humans, we naturally want to think about how endless our life will be and how we will live for however many decades until we have white hair and many grandchildren and great-grandchildren. We want to think about how our days will go on for eternity. But that's not what David prays. He prays that the Lord would show David how short and fleeting his life is. For some reason, as far as David is concerned it is a good thing that he would be reminded about how brief and numbered his days are.

How can it possibly be a good thing to have a clear understanding and grasp of our own impending death? Well, for one thing, when we think about our own mortality we must think about the only Being that is eternal and has no beginning and end. That Being is God himself. When we think about our own limitations in this world, we must be reminded about God's eternal existence and boundless power. Also, when we think about the end of our life, it helps us to dwell on how when we die we will be with God forever. And, though David didn't write this here, we will also be with King Jesus for all of eternity.

Our physical sufferings are a constant reminder of how limited and temporary our bodies are. The best reminder for us on our own mortality is when we are going through various trials, whether physical, psychological, or spiritual trials. Paul says it well in 2 Corinthians 4:16–18: "Therefore, we do not lose heart. Though outwardly we are wasting away, yet inwardly we are being renewed day by day." Our bodies are wasting away outwardly with each passing moment, but spiritually we are being renewed every day.

And Paul next says, "For our light and momentary troubles are achieving for us an eternal glory that far outweighs them all." So the troubles that we are going through are miniscule in comparison to the glory that we will experience when we are with Christ. And finally Paul says, "So we fix our eyes not on what is seen but on what is unseen. For what is seen is temporary, but what is unseen is eternal." So when we are going through trials, we are forced in some sense to think about eternal things and keep our eyes fixed on Christ. We recognize that we don't want to go through those earthly trials forever, and we must think about our impending passing out of this world.

4

Results of Suffering

So now we've looked at the source or origins of suffering, as well as how to suffer well when we are in the midst of fiery trials. In this chapter we'll look at some things that God intends to be produced as a result of our sufferings. God's purpose through and after our sufferings is that we may be closer to him. The sufferings that we go through are not meaningless or in vain. Rather, God knows exactly what he's doing when we are afflicted, and his purpose is that our faith may be refined in specific ways throughout and after the trials. This is a big part of how God uses sufferings to sanctify us. In this chapter are a few ways in which God sanctifies us through and after suffering.

God Refines Us in Our Sufferings

In everything that goes on in our lives, God is working it out for our good. There is no such thing as an accident or mistake. Paul writes, "In all things God works for the good of those who love him" (Rom 8:28). God is sovereign over everything that happens at all times all around the universe. Nothing can happen that is beyond God's power to stop. And, not only is God sovereign over all things that happen to us and all trials that we go through, but he is using them to purify and refine our faith. What a sweet thing to think about!

We can see a great picture of this in Isaiah 48:9–11. Here we see a sweet visual in which God is speaking to the Israelites about his love and care for them. He says, "I have refined you, though not as silver; I have tested you in the furnace of affliction" (v. 10).

RESULTS OF SUFFERING

Throughout the Scriptures the Lord compares his work in us to the refining process of a precious metal, like silver or gold. A couple similar examples of this are in Zechariah 13:9 and 1 Peter 1:7.

So an undesireable, unrefined metal in its more basic form is taken through a refining process to make the metal magnificent and precious. The refining process includes putting the metal through a blazing-hot furnace. Before going through the furnace, the metal is an unfinished and undesired product. But once it has been taken through the furnace, the metal is finished and complete. It is now ready to use or sell or wear. And God uses this picture to show about how he is taking us through a refining process, that we may be transformed from an unfinished product to a purified and refined precious product. He wants to transform us from someone who doesn't even know him to a great man or woman of God who seeks him above all things and wants to honor his name above everything else. God uses this refining process to bring us to this final magnificent product.

But a big part of this refining process is exactly what God uses to purify our faith. This is what God is talking about in Isaiah 48:10 when he says that he "has tested us in the furnace of affliction." So the Lord's means in refining our faith is to take us through the furnace of affliction. In other words, when we are having trials in our life, the Lord is graciously granting them to us that our love for him may increase abundantly and our faith in him may be proved genuine. But one of the ways that the Lord refines our faith is through taking us through afflictions.

Going through the blazing hot furnace is not enjoyable, just like going through the hardest trials in our life can make us wonder if we'd prefer death to that. But in the same way, God is focused on the resulting final product. The beginning unrefined gold is undesirable, but the final product is dazzling and glorious. And similarly we as early believers are like a baby that cannot even feed itself. But through God's slow refining of us, he transforms us into people whose light within shines radiantly to all those around.

In regards to the Lord refining the Israelites' hearts in Isaiah 48, the Lord talks about the stubborn hearts of the Israelites. The

SECTION I: BIBLICAL PRINCIPLES ABOUT SUFFERING

Lord desired to refine them, but it wasn't happening because of the hardness of their hearts. The Lord concentrates on their rebellion, rather than on their obedience. He delays pouring his wrath on them, because he wants them to be saved and hence to glorify him. The Lord desires to refine their hearts, but they reject it. In the New Testament, however, the Lord can refine our hearts to a different extent than in the Old Testament.

In the New Testament, genuine believers have the indwelling Holy Spirit in them. In other words, when we first have true repentance and belief in Christ, we receive the Holy Spirit in our hearts. And the Spirit will sharpen us, as each day we are "being transformed into Christ's likeness with ever-increasing glory" (2 Cor 3:18). The refining process now is different than it was in the Old Testament. Our hearts as believers are still often hard to God, just like with the Israelites in the book of Isaiah. But there is a different extent in which God refines us in the New Testament, namely, through the Holy Spirit dwelling in our hearts. And God will follow through in sanctifying us through the power of the Holy Spirit. God "is faithful and he will [sanctify us]" (1 Thess 5:24).

A great verse in the New Testament that has a similar idea as Isaiah 48:9–11 is 1 Peter 1:7. The previous few verses in the chapter are talking about God's protection of our inheritance in heaven. Then it mentions how, though we can greatly anticipate the inheritance in heaven, we still must go through many trials as long as we're in this world. Then the climax of this section of verses is found in verse 7: "These [trials] have come so that your faith—of greater worth than gold, which perishes even though refined by fire—may be proved genuine and may result in praise, glory and honor when Jesus Christ is revealed."

What verse seven is essentially saying is that God's intent in our trials is that through those trials our faith and love for Christ may grow in leaps and bounds. These trials are not simply an accident or a sign of God's neglect of us. No, quite the contrary. God's will for us in our trials is that through those trials our faith may be proved genuine. When we profess to love God and consistently go to church, that is one thing. But when we continue to sing praises to him in the midst of and after our sufferings, our professed love for him is proven as genuine. No one in their right mind would do this if they didn't really love God. So certainly it is like a test to see if someone's professed love for God is genuine.

In the second part of verse 7, there is also a reference about gold being refined. And what Peter is writing about is that our "faith may be proved genuine and may result in praise, glory and honor when Jesus Christ is revealed." Just as the blazing heat of the furnace refines the gold or silver, so God uses the fiery furnace of trials in our lives to refine and purify our faith. His desire for our trials is that through them we may bring more glory to him. His desire is that he may transform us to such an extent that people can see our lives and only attribute it to God's great power to transform us and be living in us.

Now that I am a father of two young kids, I think about particular hopes I have for my kids' lives. Of course the main one is that they may be faithful followers of the Lord. That is certainly the most important thing I may desire for their lives and pray for. My first inclination as a father of course is to wish that my children or grandchildren would not face much suffering in their lives. With that being said, I cannot deny how the Lord has used my sufferings in my life to bring me to him and increase my reliance on him. Obviously, without such sufferings I would be a completely different person. So maybe, if my wish for my kids and grandkids is that they may be faithful lovers of God, then maybe my wish for their lives should be that they do not live a life with relative ease and calm, but rather a life that has many sufferings that bring them to a complete reliance on God.

Suffering Increases Our Thirst for Heaven

When we are going through sufferings, it shows us how temporary our lives are and how weak our physical bodies are. We are called to not focus on earthly things, but rather on things of eternal value. This is what Paul writes about in 2 Corinthians 4:16–18. He talks about how our outward body is constantly

SECTION I: BIBLICAL PRINCIPLES ABOUT SUFFERING

wasting away. But Paul says that inwardly we are being constantly renewed. Any of the "light and momentary trials" currently in our lives are miniscule compared to the glory that awaits us in heaven. So Paul concludes that we are to fix our eyes not on what is seen but on what is unseen. What is seen will be burned up in the fire, but what is unseen is eternal and will never be destroyed. This should be how we live our lives.

Jesus understands this concept when he talks with his disciples about heaven to comfort them in a time of great distress. At the end of John 13, Jesus tells the disciples that he is about to leave and that where he goes they will not be able to follow him. The disciples have been following him for a few years and are frightened and distressed by Jesus' words that they soon will no longer be able to follow him anymore.

But at the beginning of chapter 14, Jesus addresses their troubled hearts and uses some simple words to comfort them: In the Lord's home there are many rooms, and his disciples will all be living together in these rooms for eternity. Jesus will come back soon and bring his disciples with him to dwell with him and the Lord forever. Thus, the disciples should be comforted. Yes, their great teacher and Savior Jesus is leaving now and they cannot follow him. But they should be comforted to know that, regardless of what suffering they face on this earth, their inheritance in heaven is to dwell for eternity with Jesus and God.

Another example of how thinking about heaven in times of distress should comfort us is seen in 1 Thessalonians 4:13–18. Paul writes about the end times when Jesus will return and bring with him those believers who have already died. And those believers who are still alive will be taken up with Jesus. Christ will return with a loud command and trumpet blast. And then those believers who have already died and those still alive will all be taken up to heaven with Christ. And we will all be with the Lord forever.

So Paul is talking about the events that will happen when Christ returns and we dwell with him forever. And Paul's conclusion on the matter is profound: "Encourage each other with these words" (v. 18). So when our hearts are troubled, we are to first be encouraged with the promise that Christ will return and will take us with him to dwell with him in heaven forever. It should cause us to have an insatiable thirst for heaven, that we may no longer be consumed by thinking about all of our earthly troubles or possessions. Rather, we are to "set our hearts on things above, where Christ is seated at the right hand of God" (Col 3:1).

And not only that, but we are called to encourage others with these words (1 Thess 4:18). We should be regularly encouraging others in the church by telling them about how Christ is coming soon. When is the last time you said that to one of your brothers or sisters in Christ? This should be a common practice, that we may be able to constantly remind one another of this amazing truth: Christ is coming back.

When we suffer on this earth, we can yearn for that day when we will be in the new heaven and the new earth, dwelling together with Christ Jesus, God the Father, all believers from all the ages, and all the legions of angels. God will wipe every tear from every eye, that there may be no death or mourning or crying or pain. When we are going through any kind of sufferings in this body, we long for the day when all of them will be taken away from us. This will not happen in this life, but only in heaven.

When We Suffer, We Often Feel Closest to God

We may think the best thing for us at any given moment is that our lives are lived without any major complications or trials. But the Lord usually has another will for us. His will for us is that we grow closer to him. He understands that this is very difficult when everything is going well in our life.

Peter writes, "Since Christ suffered in his body, arm yourselves also with the same attitude, because he who has suffered in his body is done with sin" (1 Pet 4:1). So as Christ suffered in his body, we are to be willing to suffer in our body, because if we have suffered in our body we no longer are controlled by sin. And Peter explains this a little more in the next verse: "As a result, he does not live the rest of his earthly life for evil human desires, but rather for the will of God" (v. 2). If we have suffered in our body, we don't think so much about satisfying our human desires.

Rather, as through our own trials we recognize the fallen state of the universe, we must lift our eyes to the spiritual world. We are thus more interested to please God with our lives, rather than trying to seek worldly pleasure. I can certainly relate to this a bit. When I am going through particular trials in my life, I feel completely helpless on my own. That is when I look toward God to give me strength, because I am struggling so much and can recognize my own limitations and weakness. But when things are going well for me, it's hard for me to keep my eyes on Christ. In those times I feel like I can conquer the world on my own and don't need God's help anymore.

When I am in a time of trial, I pray to the Lord with great fervor because I literally must cry out to him for mercy on me. In such times, I cry out to him in worship time and dig deep into his Word for comfort. But when times are going well, often I feel a little dull towards the Lord. I don't have any urgency or desperation in my daily pursuit of him. I may continue to spend time in prayer and in the Word each day during such times, but my heart is not as earnest in daily seeking after him.

This seems to be one design of God for the suffering he puts in our lives. He wants us to thirst and long for him, and he knows that such yearning for him is quite difficult as long as everything is smooth sailing. So it is a kind of gift or grace that God gives to us. Again, he is infinitely wise and good, so in his goodness and wisdom he gives us the lot in life that will help us draw closer to him and yearn even more for him. So when we suffer, we should be thankful to the Lord because we know his intent for us in our sufferings is that we may literally cry out to him for our salvation.

Comfort Others with the Comfort we Received from God

In the sufferings that God gives to us, he desires that through those sufferings we may be used to bless other Christians. This is exactly what Paul talks about in 2 Corinthians 1:3–6. Paul's words are quite simple: God is the God of comfort. He comforts us in our sufferings so that we can comfort other believers who are going through the same sufferings that we've been through.

So when we are suffering, God comforts us. For example, maybe I've been fired from my job. I feel in great distress, but the Lord comforts me and gives me strength. Then soon after that I hear about a friend who has also been fired from his job. Because of my experience being fired from my job, I can relate to how it feels. Not only that, but I can comfort him by directing him towards thinking about God's sovereignty and provision through it all. I can encourage him to pray for the Lord's guidance on what to do next in his life. I can earnestly tell my friend these things because I have gone through the exact same trial as him.

I can understand how he feels and the fears and insecurities that he may have as a result of his firing. It may bring lots of financial stress upon him and his family. I can also understand about how he may feel a strong sense of failure, that he has let people down and disappointed everyone. I can remember clearly about how not too long ago I went through the same thing and felt the exact same way. But God encouraged me and carried me through those same trials. I know how the Lord has been faithful to me, even through the darkest times. I can help my friend to keep his eyes focused on Christ to persevere through the hardship.

When the Lord blesses us to be able to show compassion and love towards someone who is going through the same kind of suffering that we ourselves have been through, it is a sweet gift to us because it also binds our hearts together with that person. We have been through similar trials as them. The Lord is slowly but surely showing his faithfulness to both of us. It may be similar in some ways in the bond that builds when we go through a war together with someone. Getting scars and bruises together on the battlefield can bring us so much closer. When times are desperate, we must cling to one another.

So God does not arbitrarily put trials into our lives. He knows what he's doing. He not only has absolute control over those trials, but he knows how those trials will help us in connecting more deeply with other brothers and sisters. A big part of being able to be used by God to bless others is that we are willing to tell others about our sufferings. If I never tell anyone about my trials, how can the Lord use someone to comfort me? And I may never know about how far it can go to encourage others if I were to simply share about the Lord's faithfulness to me through a particular situation. And if I open my mouth, I'll find out that someone at this moment is actually going through the same thing I went through. And they can be greatly encouraged by what the Lord taught me through those things.

But if I never open my mouth, and just simply keep everything stuffed inside, I'm withholding blessing from them and also from myself. The potentially sweet connection I could make with them I am making completely impossible. The Lord desires for us to use vulnerability within the church, that we may be open about things going on with us. We open the door for the Lord to comfort us through others, and for us to comfort others that are going through the same trials we've been through. This is a huge design in the sufferings God gives us.

We Are Forced to Rely More on God, Rather than on Ourselves

In 2 Corinthians 1 a profound truth immediately follows what is mentioned above in verseses 3–6 from Paul's words about comforting others with the comfort received from God. Paul mentions the hardships they suffered in Asia (2 Cor 1:8). They were "under great pressure," even to the extent of being "far beyond what they could endure." This pressure was so great that they even despaired of their own life, and they felt deep in their hearts the sentence of death (2 Cor 1:8–9). So Paul and his colaborers were feeling intense pressure, even to the point of despair and feeling the weight of imminent death on their shoulders. The pressure that they were feeling was way beyond what they could handle. In fact, they were certain that there was no way out of this bind. They felt hopeless and completely burned out and ready to throw in the towel and give up in this life.

Why would God put Paul and the others there in such a desperate and hopeless situation that they would not be able to handle all of the stress that they went through? The reason God would leave them in such a desperate and hopeless situation is expressed in these words: "This happened that we might not rely on ourselves but on God, who raises the dead" (2 Cor 1:9). This is a huge purpose for God in our sufferings.

One of God's greatest purposes for us in our sufferings and in our weakest moments is that we may get to the point where we properly understand we can no longer rely on ourselves. All of our strength and plans and ideas are completely useless at that point. We literally have nothing else to give. Our best efforts are completely spent. We feel we have not another ounce of energy or strength to give. We long ago eclipsed the boundary of what we thought we could handle. Our hope in our own strength is completely gone.

And it is at this point of us feeling hopeless and entirely powerless that we have no other option but to cry out to the Lord for strength and mercy. We have so fully extinguished our strength and failed in our own efforts that we must look up to the One who has no limitations to his strength and whose efforts are never impeded. He is the One who has strength to create the universe with his command. And he rules every square inch from one corner of the cosmos to the other. It is impossible for him to run out of steam, or to completely and entirely hit the wall and have a breakdown.

In Paul and his companions' situation in Asia, the Lord delivered them from their impending deaths, and will continue to deliver them (2 Cor 1:10). When we are in desperate situations, even if those situations are not necessarily life-threatening like Paul's, the Lord will deliver us. It does not necessarily mean that we will get out of our trials totally scratch-free and unscathed. But it does mean that he will carry us through those trials to the very end. And Paul tells us elsewhere that even in death we are not separated from Christ (Rom 8:38–39). Even if our trials result in our death or in our bodily harm, the Lord remains with us. It is in desperate times that the Lord carries us in his arms. We must just lay quietly and let him take the load on his shoulders. We have already realized that our own efforts will not sustain us. Only in desperate situations can we see how weak and feeble we truly are.

Later in the book of 2 Corinthians, Paul again writes about our weakness in our sufferings, and how we are fragile but God is strong in us. Paul writes, "We have this treasure in jars of clay to show that this all-surpassing power is from God and not from us" (2 Cor 4:7). What Paul is writing here is a bit similar to what he wrote in 1:8–9 about us feeling weak and helpless so that we must rely on God and not ourselves. Here in 4:7 Paul is writing that our weak bodies, minds, and spirits are constant reminders to us that the power that comes from the gospel "treasure" inside of us is from God and not from us.

Paul continues, "We are hard pressed on every side, but not crushed; perplexed, but not in despair; persecuted, but not abandoned; struck down, but not destroyed" (2 Cor 4:8–9). This is similar to Paul's words in 1:8–9 that they were "under great pressure, far beyond [their] ability to endure, so that [they] despaired even of life. In [their] hearts [they] felt the sentence of death." We feel completely annihilated and beat up. And it is in such a state that we are forced to rely on God, and not on ourselves.

A story from the Old Testament of someone relying on God in a desperate time is seen in 1 Samuel 30 about David and his men. They all saw that their wives and kids had been taken captive, including David's family (v. 3). So they all wept aloud until they had no strength to weep (v. 4). Then David's men, in their moment of great distress and heartache, started to discuss potentially stoning David. Of course this caused David to be crushed in spirit, as his men were seemingly turning against him. But even in these tragic circumstances, the Lord carried David through this trial. David was not able to make it through on his own. But his strength in the greatest trial came through the Lord his God (v. 6).

RESULTS OF SUFFERING

When We Suffer, We Are Greatly Blessed

One idea that is very prevalent in the Bible is that when we suffer, we receive great personal blessing. This may seem entirely counterintuitive. It is logical for us to think that if we do not suffer, then we are blessed, and if we suffer, then in no way are we blessed by that suffering. But, though this may be the way that we logically think, that's not what the Bible teaches us about suffering. Rather, when we suffer, we receive great reward.

The first relevant text to look at is James 1:12. James writes that we are blessed if we persevere under trials. And how exactly can we be blessed in our trials? When we persevere under trials, we receive the crown of life that God has promised to us. We will not literally be wearing a crown on this earth. But there is a reward that we receive when we persevere under sufferings. Maybe part of it is some rewards in heaven that we will receive. Maybe the crown of life is referring to our salvation: that through those sufferings our salvation is even steadier and has stood the test of the flame of affliction. Whatever the crown is, the point is that there is a reward of great significance that comes from persevering through trials.

This same idea of rewards coming as a result of persevering through sufferings is expressed by Jesus in Luke 21:17-19: "All men will hate you because of me. But not a hair of your head will perish. By standing firm, you will gain life." Jesus is talking in this section about the end times. He mentions how his followers will be persecuted because of his name. But Jesus assures the disciples that though their bodies may be killed, not a hair on their head will perish and they will "gain life." And the context of Jesus' words in Luke 21 is that his followers' dearest family and friends will betray them, even to the point of death (v. 16). Jesus also speaks of the destruction of Jerusalem and how it will be put to the sword (v. 24).

All of these words by Jesus to his disciples must have been terrifying to them. The listeners must have been tempted to be very anxious and fearful about all of Jesus' words. But the key of Jesus' words is that even when many of the disciples are killed and persecuted in these terrible ways, they will not be separated

SECTION I: BIBLICAL PRINCIPLES ABOUT SUFFERING

from God. They will not be alone in their trials. In fact, through persevering through all of these trials, they will "gain life." Certainly their reward is partly talking about the personal spiritual growth of these disciples because of their sufferings while they're still alive. But it seems that Jesus' words in Luke 21 that they will "gain life" are primarily pointing to their inheritance and reward in heaven that will come through their faith and perseverance through sufferings. This seems to be similar to what James 1:12 is saying, that when we persevere through sufferings we receive a reward from the Lord.

Another passage in the New Testament that mentions the reward that comes to the believer when we persevere through sufferings is in James 5:10–11. Again, James is writing about the reward and blessing that comes from suffering. James writes that the prophets are a good example of those who had patience in the face of suffering. Then he writes about the example of Job persevering through sufferings. In the middle of all this James writes, "We consider blessed those who have persevered" (v. 11). The Lord brought about great blessing for Job at the end of his life, after he had persevered through incredible sufferings. Of course we may not always receive material blessing like Job did by persevering through sufferings. But certainly the much greater blessing for us—and for Job—would be the spiritual blessing that comes from suffering.

In Psalm 119:67, 71 the writer hits the nail on the head about another aspect of reward coming from persevering through sufferings, which is the reward we receive now on earth because of our sufferings. He writes, "Before I was afflicted I went astray, but now I obey your word ... It was good for me to be afflicted so that I might learn your decrees." What the psalmist is getting at here is that his afflictions caused him to know God. Before his afflictions had come, he did his own thing and didn't care about God or his word. But once he was afflicted, he began to obey God's word.

And he says that it was good for him to be afflicted so that he could learn to follow God's word. If not for the sufferings that came upon him, he may have never turned to God. The Lord used the mentioned sufferings to point the psalmist to him. And all of these things were ultimately for the good of the psalmist. He was blessed and rewarded spiritually. Though he had to endure the terrible pain of affliction, it was worth it for the best possible reward, which is to have a relationship with God in the first place and to slowly grow in knowledge of him. These are of much greater value than anything in this world. That's why it was considered by the psalmist to be good for him that he was afflicted.

Section II

My Sufferings

Introduction

Is it okay to write a whole book about the topic of suffering and specifically some of my own sufferings? Why not just dwell on the more pleasant parts of our lives? Well, the simple answer to that question is that God uses the sufferings in our lives to purify us that we may know him better and bring more glory to his name. For me, and for all other believers as well, I would not be where I am now without all the sufferings the Lord has put in my path.

Some people wonder what exactly constitutes sufferings. Would it include a sore back? Or a sick wife? Or a discouraged heart? According to the Scriptures, what exactly would be accurately described as a "suffering"? I mean, most of the early Christians went through incredible sufferings for their faith, including persecution, imprisonment, execution, torture, etc. How many of us can even relate to that? I've never been imprisoned, tortured, or seriously persecuted for my faith. I've never even been openly ridiculed or jeered at for my faith. So how can I even relate to what someone like Paul went through? Do verses in the New Testament related to suffering apply to us if our life is not literally put on the line for our faith?

Well, to answer that question we can look at 2 Corinthians 11:16–33, where Paul is boasting about his sufferings. Paul gives a specific list about many of the things he has suffered over the years as a minister of Christ Jesus. We may think that everything that Paul lists will be a direct result of others persecuting him. But that

SECTION II: MY SUFFERINGS

is not the case. He mentions some things related to direct persecution, like about how he has been imprisoned, been flogged to the point of death, been beaten with rods, and been stoned. He's also been persecuted by both the Gentiles and the Jews. All of the sufferings above are those that come from intense outward persecution. This makes up only part of Paul's list of sufferings.

But that is not the end of Paul's list of sufferings. It is not only the intense persecutions that Paul lists on his list of sufferings. That is only a part of the list. So what else does Paul include in his list of sufferings? One thing to note about these sufferings listed below is that they have nothing to do with outward persecution. They are just trials that the Lord gives to Paul as a natural part of his life. Paul says that he was shipwrecked three times. He spent a night and a day in the open sea. Being shipwrecked has nothing to do with outward persecution. We might just say he had "bad luck." We have mentioned how in our sufferings there's no such thing as "bad luck" or "coincidence." Rather, the Lord knows exactly what he's doing and nothing just happens by accident or mistake. We'll look at that more in detail in a later section.

So looking back at Paul's list of sufferings, we can see that many of the sufferings he lists are not related to persecution from others. Persecution from others is not the only form of trials that we have that can be considered as sufferings. He has been in danger from rivers and in danger at sea. We can't really relate to that, as most of the modern transportation is more reliable than it was in Paul's time. Another suffering listed by Paul is that he has labored and toiled and has often gone without sleep. Certainly we have known also about laboring to the point of exhaustion. Paul says he has known hunger and thirst and has often gone without food. He has been cold and naked. These last two we really haven't experienced in this day and age. Rarely are we without food or clothes or a warm place to sleep.

One scary trial that my wife and I faced several years ago was that we were trapped in a revolting Muslim country we were visiting. I go into more detail about the story in a later section. A few days after we arrived in the country, there was a great

SECTION II: MY SUFFERINGS

revolution and the leader of the country was overthrown. Many hundreds died during the revolution. The successful revolution in that country led to many other uprisings in other Muslim countries. And we were caught right in the middle of it. And we didn't even know anyone there to help us. We couldn't speak the language. We'd never traveled to that part of the world before. The Internet was shut off by the government during the revolution, so we couldn't contact family and friends to tell them how we were doing. We were stuck in the country and we couldn't get out. Paul didn't list anything like this in his list of sufferings, but we do know that Paul faced riots on occasion, and that he was even the focus of a riot in Ephesus in Acts 19. We were certainly not the focus of the riots in the Muslim country at that time, but we were mere witnesses to the chaos.

The last thing mentioned by Paul in his list of sufferings was the pressure that he felt about the churches he had helped plant in various cities (2 Cor 11:28–29). When there was strife and conflict in the church, it grieved Paul. When there was sin in the church, his heart was deeply sorrowful. When believers that he loved so much and invested so much time and energy into were struggling spiritually, he felt the burden as well. I cannot say that I've ever planted a church, but I can still relate to Paul's words. When those believers that we love so much and have invested so much into are straying from the faith or have stopped going to a local fellowship, it really grieves us.

When a dear brother or sister is really struggling spiritually or with his or her spouse or family, we carry that burden as well. It may even cause us as their mentor-type to feel down or discouraged, as though we are experiencing this trial ourselves. As our hearts are bound with theirs, we feel pain when they feel pain. This was a real suffering for Paul. It hindered him in some capacities. Certainly he had to fight for joy when he felt discouraged about dear brothers and sisters struggling. But this is just part of investing with all one's heart and soul into people. There will be pain that goes along with it. And often, this pain can be a real suffering.

SECTION II: MY SUFFERINGS

So using the same standards as Paul does in his list of sufferings in 2 Corinthians 11, we can consider really any kind of trial that we are going through to be a suffering. We can't think that we can't relate to Paul's sufferings at all because we've never been tortured or thrown into prison because of our faith. Certainly there are parts of Paul's letters that are specifically talking about suffering through persecution. But most of what is mentioned by him is quite relevant for us to comfort us as we are going through trials.

In thinking about the sufferings I've been through over the years, the main purpose is not simply to praise the Lord for sustaining me through such difficulties. Rather, the intent is to see how the Lord has refined my faith through my sufferings. The refining process has included him maturing my faith and my knowledge and love for him as a direct result of the sufferings I've been through.

So for everything I write about in this part of the book, it is not just looking at the events themselves and how the Lord brought me through them. I also write about at least from my very limited perspective what the Lord taught me through those events. We know that "in all things God works for the good of those who love him" (Rom 8:28). So in every little circumstance that is happening at any moment all around the universe, the Lord is working each of those things out for the good of those who love him. So at any moment there are an infinite number of things going on in the universe, with the Lord having a purpose behind all of them. We usually have no idea what is going on around us, but the Lord always knows what he is doing and has a purpose for everything he does. As he says, "As the heavens are higher than the earth, so are my ways higher than your ways, and my thoughts than your thoughts" (Isa 55:9).

The Lord sees the big picture of how what he is doing will bring him the most glory. But only God can know exactly why he does everything and exactly what his purposes are at any given moment in time. We may be able to see a little glimpse about how the Lord worked things out around us for our own good. So I can share from my limited perspective how the Lord refined my faith

SECTION II: MY SUFFERINGS

through my sufferings. In looking at my own sufferings, I also encourage you to consider the Lord's purpose in your life. Think about your personal sufferings and how he wants to change you and mold you through them.

When we face trials, we can never think that these things are simply "by accident." Rather, these trials have not come to us apart from God's will and beyond his control. The Lord has infinite purposes for our suffering, even if it happens to be suffering that is a result of our own sin. And we saw in Romans 8:28 that God works out everything that happens around the universe at each moment for our ultimate spiritual good.

In the Old Testament we can see a great story that exemplifies Romans 8:28 in which a person of God is sinned against by his brothers and discarded as dead and sold as a slave. Nonetheless, through this entire trial God is ever-present and faithful to this man. These seemingly awful things that are happening to this person of God are not accidental. Rather, God uses these sins by his people against this man for God's own glory.

Many readers recognize the story I'm referring to as being the story of Joseph being sold into slavery by his jealous and hateful brothers. Joseph becomes a slave in Egypt. But through many circumstances, and God working behind the scenes in Joseph's life through the hardest of trials, Joseph goes from slavery and prison to becoming as powerful in Egypt as Pharaoh himself. Because of this, when Joseph's starving family comes to Egypt to find food in a time of great famine, Joseph is in a position to save his family with food. Joseph has forgiven his brothers for their previous sins against him, and he has mercy on them by providing them with food and giving them everything they need.

At the end of this story, Joseph is able to see the big picture about what God has been up to for all of these years. Joseph says, "God sent me ahead of you to preserve for you a remnant on earth and to save your lives by a great deliverance. So then, it was not you who sent me here, but God" (Gen. 45:7–8). So Joseph recognizes that even in the horrific sin of his brothers, God was still ultimately sovereign over sending Joseph to Egypt. And

SECTION II: MY SUFFERINGS

God's purpose in this was to save his people during this time of upcoming famine. And also of course it leads to the Israelites eventually becoming slaves in Egypt, and God being able to show his great power and glory over Egypt through his deliverance of the Egyptians out of Egypt. So Joseph being sold as a slave to Egypt by his brothers was a key part of this much larger picture of God's purposes in the world.

This same idea is spoken also by Joseph to his brothers at the very end of the book of Genesis: "You intended to harm me, but God intended it for good to accomplish what is now being done, the saving of many lives" (Gen. 50:20). His brothers certainly are not excused for their sin against their brother. But just as God used Satan's attacks of Job for Job's own ultimate spiritual good, so also did God use Joseph's brothers' betrayal of Joseph for the greater spiritual good of Joseph and his family.

This story of Joseph and his family perfectly portrays God's fulfillment of Romans 8:28 to literally work through all things and all circumstances for the good of his own people. Elsewhere Paul writes about this idea in a different way, that God "works out everything in conformity with the purpose of his will" (Eph 1:11). Paul again is writing that in all things that have happened—all over the universe and through the course of all generations of people over the ages—God works things out according to his will. As is written in the Old Testament in the book of Isaiah, "From ancient times I am he. No one can deliver out of my hand. When I act, who can reverse it?" (Isa 43:13)

God's will is unchangeable. What he wants to do, he will accomplish. This is why we can rest in things going on around us, and present circumstances in our life that seem out of control or impossible to solve. None of these things are beyond God's mighty hand to resolve or work through. My sharing of my own sufferings in this part of the book can further give testimony to God's working through all trials in my life for my own ultimate good. My stories are just small pictures of this truth.

5

Disease

THE LARGEST SUFFERINGS I have experienced in my life have been connected to disease in my family. As we have learned that God is sovereign even over terrible diseases, we know that the Lord has some purposes related to disease in my family. These things should not be seen as a sort of "accident" or "curse" to our family. Rather, God wants to use the disease in our family to achieve his purposes around us. That being said, the disease in our family has caused much heartache and pain, and continues to cause much heartache and pain. Even having some sense of understanding of God's sovereignty over diseases, actually dealing with this reality in our real lives is hard.

Disease in Family

When I was in early middle school, my mother started having some strange symptoms. She would easily feel dizzy and couldn't drive anymore after a bad car accident. She also was losing muscle control. She would kick her legs around uncontrollably and she had constant twitches. We knew that something was not normal, but no doctor could figure out what was wrong with her. My freshman year in high school, finally a neurologist suggested she fly to California to get tested for a specific neurological disease, called Huntington's disease. So my mom and dad went there together. The results later came in saying that she did in fact have this neurological disease called Huntington's disease.

The Lord used my mom's disease to help draw me to him. When I heard of my mom's diagnosis, I became incredibly depressed and spent many hours each day looking at pornography. At that time, I was still a freshman in high school. I continued in this state really through the rest of high school. However, early in high school as I was feeling particularly depressed and hopeless, I realized that I could no longer try to fight through life alone. I realized the emptiness of my life. At my lowest point, the Lord began to slowly awaken me. I started going to a Bible study on Wednesday nights, mostly because my friend promised me we'd play basketball together afterwards.

At this Bible study I soon became close to the youth pastor who led the Bible study, as well as with the other high school guys who went. For the first time in my life, I started to read the Bible on my own a bit and ask lots of questions about it. I continued in this state for another five years, still not truly committing to the Lord. Finally when I was in college I fully put my trust in the Lord and truly became a new creation in him. It was certainly my mom's disease that first awakened me to the Lord. I can honestly say that if not for this disease in my family, I may have never come to faith in Christ. And even since turning to Christ about fifteen years ago, I can see how the Lord has used the disease to continue to sharpen and purify my faith in him. So certainly I believe with all my heart in the Lord's sovereignty over all of these things, that they are no accident. Even something as seemingly terrible as an incurable disease is still ordained by our good God, who works out everything for our good.

I remember my dad telling me that there was no cure for this disease, so it was almost certain that my mom would continue to get worse until she finally died. Sure enough, that's what happened. Later while I was in high school she was having too much trouble staying with us at home, so she was put into an assisted living center. Then a few years later as her disease got worse, she was put into a nursing home. She was in the nursing home for a few more years, until she finally died in January 2007, in the middle of my second year living in China.

The Lord's sovereignty had me home from China when she passed away, and my dad asked me to preach at her funeral, which

I willingly did. The Lord carried me through my mother's death and my preaching at the funeral. I preached about the Lord's sovereignty over every circumstance in our lives, including things we think very terrible in life, like disease. According to Romans 8:28, the Lord works out everything in our lives for the good of those who follow him. This is a good promise to remember when going through great trials.

My close college friend Eric happened to also be home from China when my mother passed away, as his mother had passed away from cancer just a few months before my mother. His mom's passing was an incredibly difficult time for him, but just three months later the Lord used Eric to comfort me while my mother was near passing and as we went through everything after her death. I could really see Paul's words in 2 Corinthians 1:3–6 played out. There Paul talks about how God comforts us in our troubles, so that we can comfort others who are going through the same trials as us.

In this instance, the Lord had carried Eric a few months earlier after his mom passed away. For the most part, Eric was alone in this grieving process, at least not near his church community or family. But when my mom passed away a few months later, Eric could completely relate to everything I was going through. He could pray with me with genuine tears and sorrow, and have true brokenness for my family. So because the Lord had comforted Eric when he went through his trials with his mom's passing, Eric was able to then comfort me when I was going through the same trials.

So certainly when we are going through trials, we must consider that God desires that through these trials we may be able to comfort others who are going through the same trials. If we are silent about the trials we are going through, we are missing out on a great opportunity. The same is true if we are struggling with a particular sin. We cannot just hold these things inside us. When we are going through trials or struggling in our fight against sin, we must open up and be vulnerable to others about them. Maybe the Lord will use others to comfort us, or maybe we will find out that we can comfort or encourage others who are going or have gone through similar things. The Lord does not give us trials accidentally. He is an infinitely wise and good God, so certainly he has intentions to further extend his glory and name when he ordains to give us trials.

Getting Tested Positive for Huntington's Disease

From when my mother was first diagnosed with Huntington's disease, our dad told us that my siblings and I all had a 50-percent chance of also having the disease, as it is a genetic disease. I just assumed that whenever I may possibly get married, then I would get tested for the disease. So in late 2008 when I was engaged to get married with Lynne, I thought that before the wedding I should get tested for Huntington's disease, just so Lynne would know everything before we got married. So we drove with my dad to Wichita to get tested. I got the results about a month later.

Before the man who showed me the results opened the envelope, I prayed aloud from Job 1:21: "The Lord gave and the Lord has taken away. May the name of the Lord be praised!" I prayed that even if I were to be tested positive for the disease, I may still be able to praise the Lord for his goodness and wisdom. So sure enough, we opened the envelope and saw the test result: I was indeed tested positive. I had dreaded that day for many years. In my mind I had always just supposed that I had the disease, so I would not be terribly disappointed and crushed if I did. Of course, growing up I still really hoped that I would not have the disease. When we saw the result, we wept together and prayed in tears.

A couple weeks later we got on a plane back to China. I wondered whether I would be so crushed by this news that I would not be able to serve in China anymore. However, things did not work out that way. It was good for my healing that I could remain in China, as that was what was so familiar to me. But that does not mean it was easy. After arriving back in China and getting back to work at the college, I felt very down and depressed. I prayed for joy. I prayed that I would not just be able to deal with having the disease. Rather, I prayed that I may be able to rejoice in the disease, to truly be able to trust that for some reason God's plan was that I would be diagnosed with this disease.

Not only that, but he desired to use these trials to build my faith. Also, he desired to grow the power of the testimony of the gospel in my heart, and that through my disease somehow his name may receive glory and honor. At the same time I was crying out to the Lord to restore my spirit and give me joy, I was hit with another physical affliction. I had to have a surgery in my small city in China, because I had a pain in my body that was getting worse. So I had the surgery and stayed in the hospital for a week. This was just a couple months after receiving the news about having Huntington's disease, so it was quite a challenging time. From this surgery I was unable to walk or teach class for a few weeks. Nonetheless, I spent time on my bed crying out to the Lord for mercy.

This surgery came just when my spiritual state was struggling the most from the news about my disease. I had to cry out for the Lord's mercy. I prayed that he would restore to me "righteousness, peace, and joy in the Holy Spirit" (Rom 14:17). I did not feel these things at all. By the time Lynne and I got married a few months later in the U.S., the Lord had restored me significantly, and has mostly granted our family "righteousness, peace, and joy" since then.

Also, since getting diagnosed with the disease, God has slowly had mercy on me to not just deal with my disease, but to rejoice in it. Sure enough, I can see even in these nine years since then how, though I have no symptoms of the disease right now, the fact that I have the disease has given me great urgency. I recognize that my mother started being affected by the disease in her mid-thirties. By the time she was in her forties, she was clearly not close to 100 percent both physically and mentally. Of course each person is affected by this disease at different times and at different rates. But it does seem sure that at some point the symptoms will begin to affect me, unless the Lord cures me of the disease or there is a cure for the disease found before I experience symptoms. I am now in my mid-thirties. I know that if I am affected by the disease anything similarly to my mom, I do not have too much more time in this world while I am mentally and physically sharp.

Many times I feel like Jesus right before he was arrested: "Now my heart is troubled, and what shall I say? 'Father, save me from this hour'?" (John 12:27). I think the Lord should remove me from my trials and make my life worry-free. I, like Jesus in this story, want to be saved from the hour of trial. But that may not be what God wants for me. As Jesus responds, "No, it was for this very reason I came to this hour. Father, glorify your name!" (John 12:28). Jesus prays that through this hour of judgment and suffering for him, God may be glorified. I pray that in my disease and in my death—whenever and however that may happen—God will be glorified.

Similarly, Paul in Philippians 1 writes about the Lord's sovereignty over his life and death, and the Lord's exaltation through it all. He writes about "Christ being exalted in [his] body, whether by life or by death" (v. 20). Paul writes, "For me, to live is Christ and to die is gain" (v. 21). What does Paul mean by these words? He continues, "If I remain in the body, this will mean fruitful labor for me" (v. 22). So Paul understands that as long as the Lord intends for Paul to remain alive, Paul will faithfully serve the Lord with all of his heart. But Paul understands that if he "departs and [is] with Christ, [this is] better by far" (v. 23). Paul knows that if he dies, he will be with God in heaven. And nothing can be better than that for Paul! But Paul also recognizes that at present it is better for the Philippian church if Paul remains (v. 24). And Paul believes that at present he will remain with them, and he will be fully devoted to their "progress and joy in the faith," so that their joy in Christ may overflow (vv. 25–26).

May the Lord help me to have an attitude like Paul's about my life and death! Paul's words in Philippians 1:20–26 show Paul's trust in the Lord's sovereignty over his life and death. God is in control for where God carries Paul as long as he is in this world, and God is over even Paul's death and when it will happen. Paul understands that his life will not be a second shorter or longer than what God wants for him. He knows that he should not fear death, but actually consider death to be gain, as it means fellowship with God in heaven. But Paul does not simply long for death, and forget about life. He understands that he has no idea about when he will die. But he does know that as long as he is alive on earth, this is an indication for him of God wanting him to continue to use all of his time and energy to spread God's name on this earth.

I can see how my own disease has given me great urgency. In 2 Corinthians 12:7–10 Paul talks about the thorn in his flesh, in which it appears that God ordained to use Satan for God's own purposes. God desires to use this thorn to keep Paul from being arrogant about the visions he had and what God has done through him. Paul pleads for God to take the thorn away from him, but God does not follow Paul's wishes. Rather, because just like a father and his love and disciplining of his child, God is most concerned about whatever our long-term best is, which is often different than what we think is best at that present moment. Our long-term best is to better know God and that our lives may most greatly glorify God. We do not necessarily know how all of this is accomplished, but God does know. So God will do everything in order that his children may better know and glorify him.

God knows that this thorn in Paul's flesh will force him to not just look at temporary things on earth, but to fully fix his eyes on Jesus and the inheritance he has in heaven. So, though Paul cries out to the Lord to remove the thorn in his flesh, God, just like a good father disciplining his child, chooses to not take away the thorn in order that Paul may be forced to continued reliance and trust in God. Paul recognizes this and is thus able to boast in his weaknesses, that Christ's power may rest on him. This is in order that Christ may be magnified through Paul's sufferings.

So Paul can boast in these sufferings and boast in the thorn in his flesh given to him by God. Maybe all of us can relate to this in some sense. We maybe can think about how we have some thorn in our flesh that keeps us from boasting in ourselves. Maybe it is something related to our backgrounds or families. Maybe it is a physical ailment in our body that somehow daily reminds us of

SECTION II: MY SUFFERINGS

our own mortality and brokenness. God desires that these thorns may humble us and keep us relying on him, rather than ourselves.

For me, the clearest thorn in my flesh has been Huntington's disease. Though I am not yet physically affected by the disease, I do think about it every day; that one day probably relatively early in my life I will begin to be affected by this disease. Not only that, but it will slowly consume my body and mind over a long period of time until I finally die. I do think about this. The Lord does not expect me to not think about this daily. But these sufferings are glorifying to God when, because of my daily thoughts about my imminent disease, I am forced to fix my eyes on Christ to give me strength, rather than putting my hope in a long life, successful career or ministry, or seeing my children live to a certain age. This thorn also helps me not be attached to the things of this world, like worldly possessions or other things that will be burned up in the fire. Rather, I desire that all of my remaining days and moments on earth will be used for serving the Lord. This is the thorn that God has given to me. Just like Paul I can cry out to him to remove the thorn, but maybe in his infinite goodness and wisdom, he will not remove it.

As a result of this thorn, I do not desire to waste a single moment on this earth. I do not assume that I will live to my 60s or 70s. My mother died at age fifty-three, and even for the decade and a half preceding her death she was not physically or mentally normal in any sense. How does the Lord desire to use me in the short time that I have left on this earth? James writes that our life is "but a mist that appears for a little while and then vanishes" (Jas 4:14). David has a sweet psalm about this: "Show me, O Lord, my life's end and the number of my days. Let me know how fleeting is my life" (Ps 39:4). I can relate to David's words. David asks that the Lord would show him how fleeting his life is. Somehow David thinks it is a good thing to be able to understand how temporary his life is.

Maybe David is praying this because he knows that if he understands how fleeting his life is, he will focus more on things of eternal value and will have more urgency to seek God. I do not know exactly why David prayed this, but I can relate to it. I can certainly understand how fleeting my life is and how numbered my days are. I do not assume that I have many healthy days left. I believe that I will not live a day longer or a day shorter than how long God wants me to live. I also believe that I will not have strong mental and physical capacities to serve him a day longer or a day shorter than he wills for me. I can trust in his sovereignty in my life in these things.

That does not mean that I do not fear death though. That does not mean that I do not have fears of my body and mind being wasted away from a disease, particularly at a relatively young age. Certainly I do have these fears. I think about these things every single day. I do have hope that the Lord who saved me and gave me faith, who has sustained me through my fifteen years of faith in him, will continue to sustain me till the end, even through disease. A good promise we have about this is Paul's words to the Philippians: "Because of your partnership in the gospel from the first day until now, being confident of this, that he who began a good work in you will carry it on to completion" (Phil 1:5–6). Sometimes people use this verse to show how if someone makes a proclamation of faith or "prays the prayer," the Lord will certainly save that person.

I do not believe that to be the correct understanding of this verse. Rather, because of seeing fruit in someone's life, the same Lord who initially saved me, will also carry out my faith until the last day. That is a good promise for me. I can reasonably have fears that when I am afflicted by disease I may somehow lose the faith or fall away, but it is the Lord who will sustain me till the last day. So when I have such fears of ending poorly, I must remind myself of how I can trust with all earnestness that the Lord will be faithful in sustaining my faith till the very end. Maybe there will be people who come to faith as a result of my disease, when I begin to be affected by it and my body and mind are deteriorating. Maybe those whom I have been praying for and sharing the gospel with over the years will be able to see God's power somehow through my disease and death. Maybe some believers will be encouraged in the faith even a little bit because of something related to my disease.

SECTION II: MY SUFFERINGS

I believe that God is sovereign over how we die: "Those destined for death, to death; those for the sword, to the sword; those for captivity, to captivity" (Jer 15:2). He is sovereign over when we die: "Man's days are determined. You have decreed the number of his months and have set limits he cannot exceed" (Job 14:6). And he is sovereign over how we die: "Jesus said this to indicate the kind of death by which Peter would glorify God" (John 21:19). None of these things are accidental or coincidental. I love the last verse mentioned above, John 21:19, about how Jesus talks about how God knows not only how Peter will die, but more specifically that through Peter's death God may be glorified. That is something sweet to think about. Regardless of how we die, whether in a car accident, or simply from old age, or from a disease like cancer, the Lord desires for his children to glorify him through our deaths. This is something all of us should strive and pray for. And later in the same chapter, Jesus says to Peter, "If I want [John] to remain alive until I return, what is that to you? You must follow me" (v. 22). Jesus again is displaying his sovereignty, even over our life and death. He has complete authority over every minute that John and the rest of us live.

The Lord is sovereign even over the birds flying in the air and falling to the ground (Mt. 10:29–31). The birds flying in the air are of nearly no value, but God still is sovereign over their life and death. How much more is he sovereign over everything that happens to his redeemed children whom he loves! We may think God ordains all of our lives except for our deaths. But that is not true. God is not absent in our deaths. God is sovereign even over the sparrows in the air falling to the ground. How much more is he sovereign over his children and our lives and deaths!

In fact, though we may think that even God is grieved in our death, the psalmist writes a short but profound statement about how God views our death, something very seemingly illogical to us: "Precious in the sight of the Lord is the death of his saints" (Ps 116:15). So God does not grieve in the death of his saints. He rejoices! How sweet is that to think about! He does not grieve at all when we die. Not only does he not grieve in our death, but

DISEASE

he rejoices. If God rejoices in the passing of one of his children, how much more should we be comforted when we think about our future death!

I pray that the Lord's mercy may be on me to fully understand some sweet promises in the New Testament about death. The Scripture teaches us that in Christ's death and resurrection he was shown to be victorious over death. And for those of us who follow Christ, through Christ's death and resurrection we also have victory over death. Peter says in his preaching at Pentecost, "God raised Jesus from the dead, freeing him from the agony of death, because it was impossible for death to keep its hold on him" (Acts 2:24). So through Christ's resurrection he not only was spared from the agony in death, but more importantly he showed that death could not hold him down. In the empty tomb, we see that Christ is victorious!

But what does Christ's death and resurrection have to do with us? Paul writes an amazing chapter about Christ's resurrection and how it relates to us. He writes, "'Death has been swallowed up in victory.' 'Where, O death, is your victory? Where, O death, is your sting?'" (1 Cor 15:54–55). So through Christ's resurrection, death has been defeated. Death no longer has its hold on Christ. And the next verse gives a great cherry on the top: "But thanks be to God! He gives us the victory through our Lord Jesus Christ." So we who believe in Christ also have victory over death. What good news! Earlier in the same chapter Paul writes, "If I fought wild beasts in Ephesus for merely human reasons, what have I gained? If the dead are not raised, 'Let us eat and drink, for tomorrow we die'" (1 Cor 15:32). But Paul is convinced that the dead are raised. He did not fight wild beasts in Ephesus for merely human reasons. He knows that everything he does has eternal significance, including saving people from the depths of hell.

And elsewhere the author of Hebrews writes that through Christ's death he "has freed those who all their lives were held in slavery by their fear of death" (Heb 2:15). So it is very normal for us as human beings to have a fear of death. In fact, our instincts in us tell us to extend our lives and protect our lives at all costs. That is how God made us. But through Adam's fall, death has come into the world. And death is unavoidable for all. But now, for those who believe in Christ, we no longer need to be controlled by the fear of death that has been with us all our life. Nope, we are freed of that huge burden! We need not fear death, because we know that we will be with Christ when we die.

And Paul in the last verses of Romans 8 gives us a great promise about Christ's amazing love for us. He writes, "For I am convinced that neither death nor life . . . nor anything else in all creation, will be able to separate us from the love of God that is in Christ Jesus our Lord" (Rom 8:38–39). How sweet is this promise! So not only do we no longer need to fear death anymore, but nothing in the universe, including our death, can separate us from the love of Christ.

I conclude this chapter by stressing that the Lord has given each of us different and unique testimonies, perfectly planned by him in his wisdom and love for us. We should recognize how unique our testimonies are and consider how the Lord wants to use our stories to encourage others and spread his glory. The Lord has blessed me with a unique testimony, with a big part of it being my mom's disease and me being diagnosed as having the same disease. In a spiritual sense, those things make me who I am. So I must be thankful for the unique testimony the Lord has given me. Through this testimony, the Lord can use me to comfort others. May I never be sad or upset about this crucial part of my testimony! If not for my mom's disease, I may have stayed a cultural believer the rest of my life, just going to church casually but having no real relationship with God.

One thing related to testimony is Jesus' words to Peter: "'When you are old, you will stretch out your hands and someone else will lead you where you don't want to go.' Jesus said this to indicate the kind of death by which Peter would glorify God. Then he said to Peter, 'Follow me'" (John 21:18–19). So Jesus has given each of us a sort of "grace" in our lives. This includes our testimonies, as well as things like how we will die. All of it is intended to glorify God. And all of it is in God's perfect sovereignty, wisdom, and goodness. For Paul, part of this grace for him was the special calling and ability God gave to him to make him the ideal person to reach the Gentiles (Gal 2:9). The Lord has given me a special "grace" unique only to me. Like Paul and Peter, may I be faithful in this unique "lot" the Lord has given me! That doesn't necessarily mean that living with such a lot will always be easy. The only way to persevere is following Jesus' words: "I am the vine; you are the branches. If a man remains in me and I in him, he will bear much fruit. Apart from me you can do nothing" (John 15:5).

6

Sufferings in Ministry

Suffering in Ministry Leadership

BEING IN A PLACE of leadership in ministry, there are bound to be many challenges that come with the territory of being a leader. It could be there are conflicts on the team or church that need to be resolved. Within a church or team sometimes the conflict involves you as one of the main characters. You wish the conflict were resolved and the team would be unified again, but it just isn't happening, regardless of how many conversations or apologies are had. Sometimes two members of the team are in great conflict and you can try your best to faithfully lead the pair towards reconciliation, but there just doesn't seem to be any progress whatsoever.

As a leader, it can be incredibly discouraging, taxing, and exhausting to see the same conflicts dragged on for many weeks or months. Everyone has seemingly reconciled and made up, then suddenly it all blows up again after several weeks or months of laying dormant. Even if the conflict involves others on the team and not the leader himself, it is still draining for the leader because he is constantly praying for the team's unity and putting much of his efforts and sweat into trying to resolve the conflict. Whether the leader in ministry is serving abroad or at home, leading a team or church in conflict is always exhausting.

Another burdensome and arduous part of ministry leadership for me is dealing with my own shortcomings and mistakes. As I've been leading various teams in China for more than ten years, for three different organizations, varying in size from three to twenty-five people, I've seen lots of good and also lots of bad. I can definitely say that I've learned much over the years. But I can also consider all of the mistakes and neglect and sin and broken promises I've been responsible for to my teammates over the years. Though I've learned much from my mistakes, that doesn't mean that I am completely competent and perfect in my leadership. I make many new mistakes regularly that I've never made before. I also repeat many mistakes that I've made many times before, being very stubborn-headed and not learning from my poor decisions from the past.

Thankfully, though, the Lord is patient. Our sanctification process is not immediate, but is ongoing, as we are being changed more and more into Christ's likeness each day. This will continue until we die. We as ministry leaders and those we are leading can all be thankful for this truth. That said, there are still things that we see from our position that just crush our hearts. If we see unresolved and persistent conflict between teammates or involving us, it is just crushing and discouraging. Sometimes we even feel like we don't want to get up in the morning that day. We don't want to go to our next team meeting or church gathering. We think it would be much easier if we weren't in our current positions in this place at this time.

Other times we are deeply discouraged and grieved when we see our own failures in leadership. We see that there are many ways that we just haven't lived up to our expectations and others' expectations for us. Maybe we had intentions to do something with someone so many times regularly throughout the year, but we just didn't follow through with our intentions and got too busy. By the time we realized our neglect, it was too late and we had lost forever any trust from those we are shepherding.

Maybe there's a list of dozens of things that we've intended to get to, but we just still haven't done it, like sending our church's offering money to the proper people or going to have alone time with someone on our team. Again, the Lord is patient with us. But when we fail and don't follow through with our intentions over and over again, it can cause those underneath us to find it to be more difficult to trust us the next time we say we're going to do something. When we recognize and see our mistakes and failures as leaders, whether we recognize them while they're going on or just in hindsight, it can cause great heartache. This is particularly the case when we see how our neglect really hurts others that we were shepherding and responsible for.

Another hardship of being a ministry leader is when we have high expectations for others under us, but they soon disappoint us as they show they really are not a good fit for the work or the team. For whatever reason, they may leave very soon after arriving. We have poured out our hearts to recruit and interview them and prepare them to come serve, only for them to leave after a very short time. This is heartbreaking and perplexing, particularly in instances in which our poor leadership does not seem to be the primary reason for the person leaving. When thinking about such people, we realize that it seems obvious that the Lord does not desire for them to serve here. But though we can understand that, it is still disappointing when we invest great effort into someone to get them there, but there is really no spiritual or relational reward at all from it. They leave at their first opportunity to get out of town. Such cases can make it harder for me as the leader in ministry to trust those I am shepherding. I fear that I will pour my energy and hearts into them, but that they will leave prematurely and I will be left feeling empty-handed.

Like I said before, being a leader in ministry is not an easy job. Whether one is a pastor in a church in the U.S. or a leader of a ministry or team overseas, it can sometimes be quite burdensome. Multiple times I have wanted to yell to God like Moses in Numbers 11, when the people are grumbling to him about not having meat to eat. Moses feels the burden of taking care of all of the peoples' needs by himself. He cries out to God, "I cannot carry all these people by myself. The burden is too heavy for me" (Num 11:14).

Depending on the season in life and the season of the ministry, each ministry leader will at some point feel like Moses in this story, that he feels the role of leader to be incredibly burdensome and impossible to handle alone. It is a big responsibility, because we as leaders have the huge task to spiritually, physically, and mentally shepherd well all those souls below us. Sometimes that can

SUFFERINGS IN MINISTRY

feel like no big deal and to be quite manageable. But other times, particularly when any troubles or conflicts come up in the team or in the leader's family or personal life, it can be a great weight on the leader's shoulders to carry the entire burden alone.

I Have Been Constantly on the Move

Paul mentions in 2 Corinthians 11:26 that he has been "constantly on the move." I know that in the original context Paul is talking about he's been in danger from others and thus has had to constantly be fleeing from place to place. I've never really been in great physical danger, with people pursuing me to try to arrest me or hurt me. But I can relate to this in some sense because we have literally constantly been moving from house to house and city to city. Since I first moved to China over ten years ago, I've lived in probably nine different apartments. All missionaries don't have the same experience as me in this regard. Many missionaries will live in the same home in the same city for many years or even decades.

I certainly wish I had not moved around so much. But we have. And I'm almost certain that if we were working in the U.S. we wouldn't have moved more than a few times over the last ten-plus years, if at all. But because of our lifestyle in China, we have moved on average nearly once per year since my wife and I were married about nine years ago. I keep thinking each year that the next place will be the one where we can finally settle down for longer, but each year there are things that come up that lead to us moving to a new apartment or city. So that is a sort of suffering that we share with Paul, to constantly be on the move and to not live stably in one home for many years.

Another suffering that goes with the territory of being a missionary is the fact that we're out of the country usually when important things happen in our friends' and family members' lives. This can be quite hard sometimes. We hardly make anyone's weddings. We miss all family reunions. During my ten years in China I was only able to celebrate Christmas a couple times with family. I haven't made any family Thanksgiving or Easter meals in over ten years.

SECTION II: MY SUFFERINGS

Since my wife and I were married about nine years ago, we've attended very few weddings for friends or family back home.

All of these things are part of being a missionary. We just won't be able to make those things like we could if we were somewhere in the U.S. Thankfully, the Lord has had me home at what seemed to be random times for a couple very important family events, like my mom's passing and funeral, and my grandfather's passing and funeral, plus my brother being hospitalized after he was the victim of a random attack several years ago. I was able to stay with him in the hospital for a few days to help him. It was unbelievable that the Lord had me home for these three important events, as usually while in China we were only home for a few weeks out of each year.

Also part of living the missionary life is that we were not able to go home as much as we would if we lived somewhere in the U.S. We could only go home once per year or so. And our time at home was usually shorter than a month and filled with meeting lots of people. So it could be a challenge for us to maintain deep relationships with people in the U.S., including our friends and family. Also our parents certainly wished they could spend much more time with our kids, but they couldn't because we were in China most of the time and very far away from them.

Before we could spend more time having our daughter Skype with our parents, but during our last year in China it was harder to do that because our daughter was in the Chinese school in the weekday mornings so it made her Skype conversations with her grandparents very short. Though we can be thankful that communication options for keeping up with loved ones from far away are much better now than they were decades or centuries ago, it still can be hard to have almost all correspondence be from the complete other side of the world. But these are also things that come with the territory of serving the Lord among the unreached in the corners of the earth.

SUFFERINGS IN MINISTRY

Getting Kicked Out of my College in Eastern China

When I was still a single guy in my former city on the east coast, at the very end of my second year living in China, I was fired from my job as teacher in the university. I was not fired because of anything related to my teaching or how the school thought of me. No, in fact I had a great relationship with the school. I loved the students and they loved me. The school was satisfied with my teaching. So what happened?

Well, in June of 2007 I had some close friends from the U.S. come stay with me for what I thought would be a few months, to help in the ministry. It was my friend Jay and his fiancé, Amanda. Unfortunately, they only ended up staying in my city for about a month, rather than three. What happened was that right after they arrived, they were being very bold in going out on campus and sharing the gospel with some of the college students, which of course was why they were there. At that time, as we had never had any security problems with the local authorities, we did not know exactly what the correct boundaries were.

Anyways, after a couple weeks of this bold sharing by my friends, someone reported them to the school president. Then over the course of the next two weeks the Communist Party officials in the school had an intense investigation. They called in all the students we'd been spending time with over the two-year period, asking if we had given them a Bible, tried to share the gospel with them, or had any kind of Bible study with them. It was an incredibly tense period. The Communist Party officials would intimidate our student friends. We were having some Bible studies with students at that time, but I think most of them covered up for us. Many of them would leave the interrogation with the Party officials in complete tears.

The result of the two-week investigation was that a handful of students had mentioned my friends as sharing more openly on the campus. So the president concluded that since Jay and Amanda were my friends, I was the responsible party. Thus, they terminated my contract with the school, effective immediately. This was crushing news for me. I really loved that school and the students there. I thought I would teach there for the rest of my life. I couldn't believe that suddenly I was unemployed and near having to leave the country because I did not have a valid visa anymore to live there.

Thankfully, after a few tense weeks, the Lord opened a door for me to teach at another university in that city. The reason all of this is significant is that I can see very clearly the Lord's sovereignty in all of this. As I mentioned elsewhere, the Lord does work out all things for the good of those who love him (Rom 8:28). When I received the news that I was fired, I was completely crushed. I knew theoretically that the Lord was sovereign over all things that happened in my life. But I still found it hard to imagine how the Lord would work those circumstances out for my good.

As it turned out, though, over the course of the next year in that city, the Lord gave me a huge heart to move further west in China, where the workers were fewer. I can imagine that if I were still working at my first school with a dream job, I never would've thought about moving to another city. But only because I got fired from that job, and worked in another school in that city where I didn't know any students, was the Lord preparing me to move west. Once I moved west that next year, in the summer of 2008, I met the woman who would become my future wife, Lynne. If I were still in my first college in eastern China, I never would have met my wife. Also, the Lord has given me seven sweet years in northwestern China. If I had never initially been fired from the first college, I never would've thought about moving to western China. Certainly the Lord is sovereign, even over the hearts of the government officials and Communist Party leaders.

Another huge way that the Lord used my firing at that university for my own good was shown the following semester in my new school in the same city. I was close to the foreign teachers there, but didn't know any of the students. I also was still slowly recovering from getting fired from my previous college, and I was still trying to maintain friendships with many of the students there. So it ended up being a slow fall semester for me. My first two years in China I was always running around meeting students, all day, every day.

But at the beginning of that third year, I felt like the Lord just wanted me to stay inside for a period. I didn't know why exactly at the time, but the Lord wanted to use that time so I could come to know him much more intimately. I started having a full day of fasting and prayer each week. I was trying to wake up early in the morning every day and spend many hours each week in prayer, Scripture memory, reading the Word, fasting, listening to sermons, and reading sweet Christian books. I really had little desire then to go out and be with people. I just wanted to stay inside and soak up time with the Lord. I was greatly encouraged by listening to John Piper sermons, particularly his "Men of Whom the World is Not Worthy" biography series. I would listen slowly through them and write in my journal any notes from them. I also read some great books then, like *Autobiography of John G. Paton*, *The Life and Diary of David Brainerd*, *The Forgotten Spurgeon*, *The Soulwinner*, and *The Biography of George Muller*.

This period of sweet alone time with the Lord lasted for about three months. It was a time of unbelievable communion with the Lord, in which I was learning deep and profound truths about him. I was learning how to daily follow him, committing all of my time to him. Looking back now, I can see how the Lord used that time to develop me in my faith for the more than ten years since then. None of these things would have happened if I had not been kicked out of my first college. Certainly the Lord is completely sovereign, even over things which we think just cannot work out for our good.

Rejection by IMB

Once I first joined a Southern Baptist church in 2008, I had it in my sights to eventually join the SBC's mission organization, the International Mission Board (IMB). I had heard that my experience in China and some connections with IMB leaders in my part of China would help me be a good candidate for the IMB. Even before my

SECTION II: MY SUFFERINGS

wife and I were married in 2009, we made plans for the future with the assumption that it would include us being with the IMB.

But the Lord had other plans for us. We started the long application process for the IMB, going through the very preliminary application. Earlier that year I had been diagnosed with Huntington's disease. So in 2010 I contacted the recruiter with the IMB and told him that we did not want to go through the whole application process, just for us to be denied at the end because of my disease. So I told him about the disease I had been diagnosed with. He spoke to some IMB doctors, and after several weeks he got back to me with the bad news that we had been rejected to join the IMB because of my disease. These developments were completely contrary to the plans we had made for ourselves. However, I had a feeling then that the Lord had some kind of plan for us that would just not be working with the IMB.

I cannot say exactly what it would be like if we were with the IMB. I know they take great care of their missionaries, so I am sure it would be good to be with them. But that is not what the Lord wanted for us. One simple purpose the Lord may have had in it was that I started doing online seminary work in 2009 at Southern Seminary because I thought I would need some basic courses to get into the IMB. Maybe if we were not applying for the IMB, I never would've gone to seminary in the first place. My seminary education at Southern Seminary and my PhD studies at Trinity have both been a huge blessing for me. Maybe if I had not applied to the IMB in the first place, I would not have experienced any of the blessings received from seminary.

Another blessing, in hindsight, of being rejected by the IMB is that the Lord just had a different path for us. The year after being rejected by the IMB, a friend and I started a small mission organization focusing on northwestern China. This would not have happened if I had joined the IMB. It has been a great blessing to see the mission organization slowly growing, and just to be able to have some sweet friendships through it. So I can see how the Lord closed one door with the IMB, while opening many other doors that otherwise would not have been opened.

7
Other Sufferings

Egyptian Revolution Witnesses in 2011

How can we possibly face sufferings while travelling? Well, in January 2011 we decided we would take a trip to Egypt. We wanted to scout out Egypt to see if there were any Chinese missionaries there. We also wanted to see what kinds of jobs may be good for any Chinese missionaries that would go there. We had Chinese believers in China who were waiting for our response to tell them about possible opportunities for ministry for them in the Muslim world. Little did my wife and I know what we were getting into.

We arrived in Cairo, Egypt on January 19, 2011. We spent some time in the city just walking around and seeing the main sites, like the pyramids. We also connected with some local Arabic-speaking believers. After several days in Cairo, we took a train north to Alexandria. It was the next day that we heard that violent riots had burst out in Cairo just the day before in Tahrir Square, with three being dead. Tahrir Square in Cairo was where we had stayed in a local hostel just a few days earlier. The Egyptian rioters were trying to overthrow the supposedly corrupt government of Hosni Mubarek, who had been the president of Egypt for about thirty years. The Egyptian rioters were trying to follow in the footsteps of the Tunisians, who had overthrown their government just ten days prior.

On January 28 the protests began in Alexandria. The previous few days had been mostly in Cairo and Suez, but that day they started in Alexandria. After morning prayers at the mosque, everyone raided the streets. We heard and saw the protestors walking up and down the streets. They seemed mostly peaceful at the time.

SECTION II: MY SUFFERINGS

Later in the afternoon we tried to get a taxi back to our hostel, which was right in the middle of the main protests. A German friend we had just met named Lukas helped us get a taxi. We drove right through the middle of all of all the protestors, maybe two thousand or so total. All of our hearts were in our throats. The sky was filled with smoke, as people started burning things. It was a terribly nerve-racking day. The army came rolling in the evening, so things died down a bit. From our hostel lobby, everyone was looking down on all the action, which was right below our window. Our hostel oversaw the main street right by the Mediterranean Sea. We bought train tickets to leave the next morning to Cairo, but all trains to Cairo were cancelled.

A couple days later we went to the airport hoping to buy plane tickets to Luxor or any other place, but again came up empty. There were huge tanks guarding the airport. We went back to the train station and got tickets to go to Cairo the next day. The protests were getting worse and worse, especially in Alexandria and Cairo. At that point, a hundred people around Egypt had already been killed in the protests. Outside our window, down on the ground, was a group of men carrying wood beams and knives and looking for trouble. All morning until 4 p.m. the city was quiet. After that it got crazier. No police were on the streets, for fear of being attacked. So the streets were a bit chaotic. The president of Egypt, Mubarek, fired his cabinet that day, but the protests wouldn't stop until he resigned. Lots of foreigners were being rushed to the airport in Cairo to fly back to their countries. The Internet had been out for a few days, so we weren't able to tell our families we were okay. I was dwelling on this verse: "Be strong and courageous. Do not be terrified. Do not be discouraged, for the Lord your God will be with you wherever you go" (Josh 1:9).

During the day the shops were open. The streets were quiet. We did lots of shopping for food. From 4 p.m. to 8 a.m. the city was on curfew. There were no police on the streets. There were just huge tanks everywhere. The army was in support of the revolution, so the tanks weren't used against the protestors, but rather to keep peace in the streets. There were men with bats outside our window

OTHER SUFFERINGS

the previous two nights. We assumed they were dangerous. Then one afternoon we talked to them outside.

It turns out they each lived on that street. They stayed outside all night to protect the streets from thugs and thieves. Each block had elected a "public government" representative. He was responsible for protecting that block. They blocked the roads and wouldn't even let taxis through. They'd say, "Even taxies *can't* be trusted!" I got a picture with three of these street vigilantes, one with a wooden post, one with a cane, and one with a knife. From our window we saw them "arresting" a couple trespassers and taking them who knows where. They took the job very seriously.

Aside from just having no police, it was reported that a few thousand inmates escaped from a Cairo prison. So all the people were pretty afraid at that point. Also, we didn't have a source of reliable information. We heard all kinds of crazy rumors on the streets. We had no Internet. The local news was all in Arabic and was controlled by the government. The only English news was based out of Iran, so they were very anti-U.S., and even the reports on protests there seemed incredibly exaggerated. So it was hard to get a good gauge on what was going on there and in Cairo.

After several days of waiting in our German friends' home in Alexandria, Lynne and I agreed it was best to try to leave Egypt as soon as possible. We accepted that no more touring or meeting people would be done. It seemed a good time to leave, as the airlines in Cairo were adding flights and making it easier for foreigners to get out. There seemed to be a couple safe ways to get to the Cairo airport from there. So Lynne and I went to get train tickets to leave the next day. Unfortunately, all trains were cancelled for the next week. So we decided to try to pay a driver LE 500 to get us directly to the airport. We had heard many reports about that day's planned "Million-Man March" in Cairo.

The people were getting more and more upset against the government. The president (Mubarak) was refusing to step down, but was rather just appointing new cabinet members. We figured the protests would begin after noon, so if we could get to the Cairo airport before noon, we would be okay. The previous day we had called the U.S. embassy again and they told us they were suggesting all U.S. citizens in Egypt to leave right then. At that point over 150 protestors around Egypt had been killed. We had driven by a huge government building and two large government vehicles in Alexandria that had been totally toasted and destroyed. And we had heard it was much worse in Cairo. This verse comforted me greatly: "He is my rock and my salvation; he is my fortress. I will never be shaken" (Ps 62:2).

On February 1, 2011 we hired a taxi driver to take us to the Cairo airport. We left at 7:30 a.m. We made it to the Cairo airport by noon, but not before going through many security checkpoints and delays on the roads. Our driver was determined to get us to the airport. And Lynne and I were praying a lot too. Upon arriving at the airport, we were lost in a sea of foreigners who were trying to leave the country. After being told a couple times that it would be one to two days before they could get us on a plane, they told us there were standby tickets for that day's 4 p.m. flight. We couldn't believe it. So we took the flight to Abu Dhabi, where we had a twenty-four-hour layover, then flew back to China just in time for the Chinese New Year on February 3.

Though these things happened over seven years ago, I am still amazed at the Lord's sovereignty in all of it. It was my first trip to a Muslim nation. We were there for only two weeks. There had not been any huge conflicts in that area for a while. Mubarak had been the president of Egypt for about thirty years. Egypt was considered a relatively stable country. The events surrounding the Arab Spring were some of the largest news events in the world for the past decade or more. What happened with the overthrow in Egypt was what caused many other Muslim countries to see similar revolutions, some also successful.

The street vendor who burned himself to death in protest in Tunisia was officially the one who sparked the protests elsewhere. But as Egypt is much more influential in the Muslim world than Tunisia, it was not until the revolts in Egypt that the idea really spread to the oppressed peoples across the whole Muslim world that it may just be reasonable and worthwhile to attempt to overthrow the regime. That part of the world is still recovering from all of those events seven years ago. I am just amazed that the Lord would have us be in Egypt when the protests and riots began. It was an incredibly stressful and frightening time when we were there and we thought we may never make it out, but now we can see the bigger picture of how those days played a huge part in world history from the past decade and beyond. And God had us there for it, and he delivered us from it.

Suffering through Intense Anxiety in Seminary

Is it really possible to suffer while in seminary? Shouldn't a seminary be the place where the most encouragement and spiritual growth occurs? Yeah, that's what I thought before we moved to the beautiful Southern Seminary campus in Louisville, Kentucky in August 2013. I was ready to take on the world. I'd taken some classes online to get a simple Master's degree there, but in the summer right before we moved on campus I decided to change to a Master of Divinity. That sounded like a great idea. The only problem was that instead of my degree requiring forty-eight total hours to graduate, it now required a whopping ninety-four total hours to graduate. So during that year of living on campus in Louisville, I had the mindset that I had to cram in as many hours as I possibly could. I also had previously signed up to do a pastoral internship at a church in Louisville, so I'd be doing that on top of all the classes I needed to take. While in the U.S. I also wanted to keep in as close of contact as possible with the workers that I was leading in northwestern China.

These things all seemed like a great idea at the time. Maybe I overestimated myself in thinking that I could successfully balance all of these things at the same time. Everything seemed to be going smooth at first, and I had lots of initial excitement about all of it. But a few months later, in mid-November 2013, I hit a huge wall. Looking back now, there were many things that I was not balancing well at all. I was not making proper boundaries with my studies. I literally would study all day every day, 7 a.m. till 10 p.m., weekdays

SECTION II: MY SUFFERINGS

and weekends. It was madness. I was cramming in so many classes that I thought that was the only way I could get through it all, to literally spend every waking moment studying, stopping only for church and class. I was taking nothing resembling a break during the day or in the week. I was also trying to balance with the schoolwork leading the work in northwestern China and doing the pastoral internship.

So in mid-November I hit the wall, which came in the form of intense anxiety. It was all strange because I had never really experienced intense anxiety in my life, and certainly not since becoming a believer in college. So it all crept up on me. During this intense anxiety time in Louisville, I had a huge fear of being around people, going to classes or even to church. It was incredibly painful. This continued for about four months. These months were some of the hardest times for my wife and me.

Part of what made these four months so hard was not only my intense anxiety, but also that we were feeling loneliness like we had never felt before. Before arriving at the seminary, we assumed that the year would be just a great period of encouragement and mentoring from older sweet brothers and sisters at the seminary and church. But we underestimated the adjustment that comes from living in a foreign country like China for so many years, and then moving to the U.S. for a year of intense studies at seminary. We missed China so much, but because of my intense anxiety we wondered if we would ever make it back to China at all. And that brought feelings of hopelessness and despair.

Though I was caught in an unmatched period of intense anxiety, I did not really make any adjustments with my studies, but just continued on going full speed ahead. It was not until the very end of January when the Lord started to slowly restore our family. He did this in the form of moving in my wife to bluntly and directly yell at me with great force. I'm thankful to have a wife who is willing to say the hard things to me sometimes. So on this occasion, she told me that our family could not continue in this way. Because of my studying all day and night for many months, I was neglecting my wife and daughter and it was really wearing on them. I was not leading them spiritually in any sense. I wouldn't even spare any time to go play with them for thirty minutes on the beautiful seminary lawn. I was just completely consumed by my studies.

And, big praise to the Lord for this, my wife's words actually sunk in. I started to think about what she had said to me. I knew that her words were truthful, but I didn't really know how to change anything. So I spent an entire day in prayer and fasting, praying specifically that the Lord would guide me on how to lead my family spiritually. Our daughter was only a year and a half old at that time, but I had been nothing but passive before that in anything related to spiritually leading my family.

Through my prayer and fasting time that day, and in the following days, the Lord slowly started revealing things to me about my neglect of my family. That night we started to do family devotionals for the first time. We had never done them before that since my daughter had been born. So I began leading my family in nightly devotionals. That was a big step in leading them spiritually. Then I started to take Saturdays completely off for "family days," which involved a full day devoted to the family. Usually my wife, daughter, and I would take the day to go explore around Louisville to an area we hadn't seen before, or to visit the beautiful parks there. When we started having family days each Saturday, my wife and daughter were so excited. All of us would see it as a big highlight of the week.

I started taking one evening a week to set aside for chat time with my wife. After our daughter was asleep, we'd just chat together for a couple hours about things that had been going on and things on our hearts. Doing this once a week significantly improved my communication with my wife. If there were important things on our hearts during the week, we would save them for our chat night, when we could talk in a loving manner, rather than under stress or completely exhausted.

Also, each Friday night after our daughter went to bed my wife and I would watch a movie or listen to a sermon together. Though we weren't actually going out anywhere, this still gave us a weekly leisurely night together. This adjustment helped us as we

SECTION II: MY SUFFERINGS

eventually returned back to China, as we were able to have something like a "date night," without needing someone around us to take care of our daughter every week for us to go out.

Soon thereafter I started to take weekends off for studying, and only studied 7:30 a.m. to 5 p.m. each weekday. In the evenings I would go walking after dinner with my family and spend more time with my wife, rather than studying in the evening. I also realized the value of taking a trip somewhere as a family and putting down all distracting things for the trip. We took a family vacation to the North Carolina Outer Banks area, our first family vacation really since my daughter had been born. I didn't do any studying or computer time during that trip.

The crazy thing about taking consistent rests from my seminary studies was that, though I continued taking an equally heavy amount of classes as before, and though I was studying probably fifteen to twenty hours less per week than I was before, I got the same grades in my classes as I was before and was able to take the same amount of classes. I learned to study much more effectively and learned how to read books and write papers more quickly. So the Lord was multiplying my time and energy and blessing my efforts when I started to realign my priorities to put the Lord at the top, and my family next, and my studies below that.

From when I started to slowly make these adjustments, the Lord slowly starting pulling me out of the rut I was in. This was not an immediate refreshing, but a gradual one. There were a few practical things I did that helped in the Lord pulling me out of the intense anxiety period. The first was to try to exercise daily. Each morning I would do about a fifteen-minute workout of pushups and situps. Though quite short, doing this every day helped me physically and spiritually. Also, I like making charts, so I kept an Excel chart in which I would keep track each day of whether I had peace, hope, and joy in the Lord that day. If I did for the most part, I'd write "Yes" in my chart. If I did not, I would write "No." This helped me in just having a very simple goal for each day, to strive from the beginning of the day to the end to fight for peace, hope, and joy in him for that day.

OTHER SUFFERINGS

Another key part of the Lord pulling me out of the pits was that I had close accountability with a few guys at our church, so I didn't just have to keep my struggles stuffed inside. I had two brothers that I would meet with at 6 a.m. each Thursday morning and we'd have accountability time together. Being able to pour out my heart to them each week and have them pray for me was incredibly powerful. If we are struggling with a particular sin (and all of us are struggling with various sins at all times), we need accountability from others. We cannot keep that sin hidden, regardless of how common we feel the sin to be. As Paul says in 2 Corinthians 1:3–6, when we don't share our struggles with others, we are missing out on great opportunities to bond with them and to receive mutual encouragement and comfort.

And maybe the most important part for the Lord refreshing me through an intense psychological and spiritual depression was to just cling to the Lord. I would need to cry out to the Lord daily for mercy, as I felt very fearful of doing any normal things I'd done all my life, like going to class, going to church, or meeting new people. I was desperate for the Lord's deliverance of me. I had great fear that I was going to remain in that same state for the rest of my life.

It seems that when we are in our most desperate times is also when we can feel closest to the Lord, as we cry out to him each day for mercy. We realize that we really cannot do anything in our own strength but must rely on his, even just to do basic daily tasks. So often we are quite capable and we think to rely on our own strength, but the Lord will bring us low and give us hardships to show that we cannot rely on our own strength, but must rely on his strength.

This is similar to what Paul talks about in 2 Corinthians 1:9 as he writes how "[feeling great despair even to the point of death] happened that [they] might not rely on [themselves] but on God, who raises the dead." What a sweet reminder this is! How easy it can be to forget this simple truth. How easy it is to try to do things in our own strength, even when we think we are serving the Lord. When we're at our very lowest points, the Lord shows us exactly how weak we are. It's not fun at all, but the

Lord desires to increase our faith through this humbling and to increase our daily reliance on him.

Suffering in Miscarriage

Three years ago we had a surprise period of suffering that completely knocked us off our feet. My wife was almost exactly five months pregnant. Everything seemed to be going well in the pregnancy and with checkups. We had planned to have the baby in our city in China, just as we had done with our daughter a few years earlier. In fact, we felt pretty comfortable in the whole process of having a baby in Chinese hospitals. Maybe we were even a little proud about it and felt like it would be a piece of cake.

However, any sense of pride that we had about an anticipated smooth pregnancy and delivery in China was completely eliminated. On April 25, after returning from a full day travelling across the city to meet with local brothers and sisters, my wife was alarmed as we were about to go to bed. She thought that something about the baby in her belly was not right. We didn't know what was coming. We didn't want to take any risks, so we had our teammates come over to watch our daughter as my wife and I took a late-night taxi to the hospital to have a checkup on the baby.

Sure enough, the doctors said that the baby in my wife's belly would not survive. We were shocked by this news because my wife was already nearly five months pregnant. Generally speaking, miscarriages will happen during the first three months of pregnancy, and not during the second trimester. How could this be happening to us? It seemed like we were in a nightmare. The Chinese doctors said it would be impossible to save the baby's life. We wanted to wait to get a second opinion, rather than expediting having the baby coming out.

The next day we got a phone call from a foreign OB/GYN doctor in a neighboring city. She had heard about our situation and that we were near losing our baby. She thought it might be possible to save the baby's life though. So she jumped into an old ambulance and rode it over three hours to our city to pick us up

OTHER SUFFERINGS

at the hospital. She arrived at our hospital room around midnight and we took the old ambulance with her on a bumpy road the nearly four hours to her hospital in the neighboring city. We didn't get any sleep that night.

We got checked into the hospital room and the doctor performed a surgery on my wife the next morning in an effort to save the baby's life. It seemed to go well initially, and the doctor was somewhat optimistic. She did tell us about the high possibility that the baby would still not survive. We were praying like crazy for the Lord to perform a miracle to spare the baby's life. The Lord, however, had different plans. A couple days after the surgery, the doctor said that my wife had contracted an infection. The baby would not be able to stay in her belly. So the doctor allowed for the baby to come out naturally, and our baby, Ann, came out. She was only breathing for several seconds, and then she was gone.

We wanted to honor our baby's life by giving her a name. We named her Ann after missionary to Burma Adonirum Judson's first wife, Ann, who also died very early in life. We believe that God is the creator of human life. Thus human life begins at the point of conception in the womb. So we wanted to honor this precious life by giving our daughter a name. Immediately after Ann's birth and passing, we took pictures with her in some clothes. Our dear friends decorated a box for us to put her in. We were thankful to be able to do all of these things to honor Ann. Even though her life was cut incredibly short, she was still a sweet gift from the Lord. We wanted to honor her as a human created by God.

A few days after her passing, our sweet friends drove us up into the norwestern China mountains outside the city so we could have a proper burial for baby Ann. We had mixed feelings about what that would be like and if we were up for the task, but we knew we needed to do it. We drove very far off the beaten path, on a road up into the mountains that was completely empty. It was a cold and rainy day. We got out the shovels and started digging right by a line of trees. Our families came with us, but sat in the car as we dug the grave. Certainly not something that any father wants to ever do in his life: dig his own child's grave.

Our friends had made a proper casket for baby Ann. We put her in the casket and had a short service for her. Through tears while the rain was still coming down, I said a few things about her. We sang a song and a few of us prayed. Then we put her casket into the hole in the ground and covered it up.

We were lonely, as we were away from our families in the U.S. during all of this. But the Lord provided support for us during this incredibly challenging time, particularly through the family mentioned above. They went so above and beyond to help us during this fall-flat-on-your-face time. Through the body of Christ, the Lord provided the comfort and help that we needed at that moment and over the next several months, as we continued to grieve our loss of baby Ann.

It took several months for the Lord to continue to heal us in any sense. I grieved a little differently than my wife. I wept hard the first day when everything first happened. And that was most of the outward grieving that I did. But for my wife, she was more stoic when everything was happening. But her tears came later. And her grieving lasted much longer than mine, as she continued to have bad days for several months after that, when she would feel overwhelmed with grief and bitterness about things with baby Ann. Immediately following the miscarriage, my wife had a couple months of intense migraines. It just seemed to be that the Lord was piling all the bad stuff on us at one time, one thing after the other.

Suffering When All Seems Well

Sometimes there are seemingly good things that happen in our lives that still can be a trial. An example could be receiving a large raise at work, which seems like a blessing, but ultimately leads to more struggles about worrying about money and possessions. Before receiving the raise, a man has thought about money very little and has felt overall content in the Lord in life. But after he receives the large raise, he finds himself tempted to covet after nice homes or cars or electronics that he sees. He finds it much more difficult to be content with the Lord and with what he has.

Another example would be if a wife is interested to find a full-time job after several years of being a full-time housewife. She finds a job that seems perfect and provides a good salary. It seems like the perfect situation. But the trial may be that the wife, after several months of working full-time, realizes that her life has now changed significantly. She is away from home more than she wants to be. And she is not able to be with her kids or husband as much as she used to be. It can be a struggle for the wife, as she may not be sure about what God wants her to do. When she is full-time housewife, she yearns to have some kind of full-time job. But when she works full-time in an office in a seemingly ideal job, she just misses her family and yearns to return to the time when she was able to spend loads of time with them.

An example of a trial in a time that seemed good for me happened about two years ago. I was comfortably living in China, minding my own business and happy to be there without any kind of planned extended time in the U.S. in any foreseeable future. But beginning in summer 2015 I did begin to think about a PhD at a seminary in the U.S. I thought that even if I did do that, I would not begin anytime soon, and I would study at a program where I could just do intensives for a few weeks at a time and remain in China. I decided to apply to a school, though I had very little thought about actually following through with it.

I was waiting to hear back from the school. I told my wife that if the school did not offer me a decent scholarship, then I would happily forget about the PhD life altogether and we would just remain in China indefinitely. I assumed that I would not get any kind of scholarship, and I would not have to be challenged with the decision of staying in China or returning to the U.S. for a PhD. But my assumptions about PhD possibilities were not accurate.

Early in March I received an email from the school saying that I had been offered a decent scholarship there. I felt excited partly as I read it, but my heart was also torn. I did not want to leave China! And the scholarship required that I stay in the U.S. at the school for two years, beginning in the fall, just several months later. This was not what I had planned on doing! My heart was very

SECTION II: MY SUFFERINGS

divided. The next morning at our foreigner church in northwestern China, my heart was heavy as I preached. And afterwards I told my teammates about the email I had received the day earlier about the scholarship from the seminary in the U.S. And with a heavy heart I burst into tears. I really did not want to leave my teammates and our lives and friends in China. This was not a part of any "five-year plan" that my wife and I had made over the previous ten years.

The next four months, which were my last months in China before moving to the U.S., my heart continued to be torn in all directions. Some days I would feel excited about the opportunities at seminary in the U.S. But most of the time I felt extremely anxious and fearful. I was incredibly emotional during that time, and I would regularly weep for various reasons. I was terrified that I would have a repeat of the intense anxiety that I had during the four winter months of my MDiv at Southern Seminary in Louisville. I never again wanted to go through such a time as that. I was afraid of the thought of being away from China for two whole years. I remembered our hardest times in Louisville, and how at some points it felt like the year was never going to end and we would never return to China. I thought that in going back to the U.S. for two years to work on the PhD, I would be willingly setting myself up again for a repeat of the struggles in Louisville.

So when I left China in July, I remained anxious and fearful. These feelings continued through the summer at home, and through the first several months at seminary. But looking back now, I can see how the Lord clearly opened the door for us to come here for this season. We could try to have another kid again. We could be closer to family. And we could meet tons of great people and learn much and grow in our faith. Looking back, there is no doubt in the Lord's hand in our coming back to the U.S. for this time. I could see that to some extent while the original door was opened before we left China, but I still continued to kick against God's will for us in this time.

This is a recent example of something that on the surface seems good to everyone around. Receiving a scholarship to do a PhD in the U.S. at a respected school is a unique opportunity.

But, that being said, this so-called good thing still brought me much anxiety and fear. It was indeed a real time of trial. It was suffering when all seemed well.

8

Conclusion

In conclusion of this book, it is helpful to look at Psalm 77:10–12, where we can see a great picture of the attitude we are to have about our trials from the past, and how the Lord delivered us from those trials. The psalmist writes, "'To this I will appeal: the years of the right hand of the Most High.' I will remember the deeds of the Lord; yes, I will remember your miracles from long ago. I will meditate on all your works and consider all your mighty deeds." We must meditate on how the Lord has delivered us in the past. We must remember the miracles the Lord has performed in our lives. We must regularly give thanks to him for these things. We can think about the desperate situations we've had in the past, and how the Lord somehow sustained us each time, even though we may have felt emotionally and spiritually on the brink of destruction. Like the psalmist, when our hearts are heavy or we feel hopeless, we are to meditate on those ways the Lord has delivered us through trials in our lives.

Also, we can learn from Jeremiah in the book of Lamentations about where his hope comes from during the darkest times: "I remember my affliction and my wandering, the bitterness and the gall. I well remember them, and my soul is downcast within me" (Lam 3:19–20). We can see Jeremiah's sadness, which in this letter is a result of the destruction of Jerusalem. This causes Jeremiah to feel bitterness in his soul, and it causes his heart to be downcast. But this downcast spirit is not the end of the story.

Jeremiah continues, "Yet this I call to mind and therefore I have hope: Because of the Lord's great love we are not consumed, for his compassions never fail. They are new every morning; great

CONCLUSION

is your faithfulness. I say to myself, 'The Lord is my portion; therefore I will wait for him'. The Lord is good to those whose hope is in him, to the one who seeks him; it is good to wait quietly for the salvation of the Lord" (Lam 3:21–26). In Jeremiah's words, we can understand how he clings tightly to the Lord through his trials. Through these trials, he has hope. He is not consumed in his trials, though he may often fear that he may be. He knows about God's great love and how his compassions are new to him every morning. His daily sustenance and strength comes from the Lord. His hope is in the Lord, so he believes the Lord will rescue him. This is what gives him such a hope through intense trials.

www.ingramcontent.com/pod-product-compliance
Lightning Source LLC
Chambersburg PA
CBHW070516090426
42735CB00012B/2804